THE
WARRIOR'S
WEAPONS

•• VOLUME ONE ••

DR. UWAKWE C. CHUKWU

DR. UWAKWE CHRISTIAN CHUKWU
Hearts of Jesus and Mary Ministries
website: www.hjamm.org
Email: ucchukwu@hjamm.org
Email: ucchukwu42@students.tntech.edu

Ordering Information
Quantity sales. Special discounts are available on quantity purchases by corporations, associations, and others.
For details, contact the "Special Sales Department"
at the information above.

The Warrior's Weapons (Volume 1)
Dr. Uwakwe Christian Chukwu—1st edition
ISBN: 978-1-64606-335-2

Cover Design & Typesetting By
Divine Studios Inc
+1.678.599.7582

Printed By
Lan Manuel Print House
8700 Commerce Park Dr #111
Houston, Texas. 77036
Email: lmphhouston@gmail.com
Tel: +1.832.367.8420

Published in the United States of America

THE
WARRIOR'S
WEAPONS

•• VOLUME ONE ••

Dedication

To My Lovely Children:
Chiemelie, Onyinyechi, Mmesomachukwu, and Ebubechukwu.
Each of whom has a special place in my heart.
You are my little prayer warriors in our home.
You shall exceed your Dad!
God bless you all,
In Jesus name
Amen!

TABLE OF CONTENTS

Acknowledgment

My foremost gratitude goes to the Holy Spirit who provided the inspiration, guidance, and grace to write this book. I thank in a very special way Miss Marie Bernadette Abe Ewongkem for her editorial expertise in taking the manuscript of this book and meticulously moderating it. I am very thankful to you!

I am utterly grateful to my Spiritual Director and mentor, Rev. Fr. Cletus Imo. He is both my father and my model. His life inspires me much. It is largely his mentoring, combined with the support I receive from others like him that keep me aflame in the faith. A million thanks cannot suffice to express my gratitude to Rev. Fr. Anthony Madu for the sacrifices he makes in sharing the Word of God weekly in our Ministry.

Many words may be said, but none is enough to appreciate the support received from my parents, Mr. Nweke-Onovo Chukwu and Mrs. Roseline Chukwu, most especially for showing me the way to God. You have no idea of the gravity of my deeply-felt gratitude for your sacrifices that brought me thus far. Mum, you are the first prayer warrior I ever knew. You laid the foundation for my prayer life. You prayed the fire of God into my life!

I have no luxury of space to thank all the passionate and caring members of my ministry—*Hearts of Jesus and Mary Ministries* (HJM)—for their unrelenting prayers for my family and ministry.

HJM family is a legion in my life, and I am filled with gratitude for their willingness in showering me with the greatest gift—prayers. I reserve a sincere gratitude to all the Board of Directors, Ministry Leaders, and Workers in the HJM Ministry, whose efforts in the ministry stir deep gratitude from my -heart.

My gratitude goes to Mr. Emmanuel Aryee for taking his time to typeset this book and for designing the cover.

I am overwhelmingly grateful to my beautiful wife, Chinyere, and our wonderful children—Chiemelie, Onyinyechi, Mmeso-machukwu, and Ebubechukwu—for making our family a happy home for all of us. This book is dedicated to the kids. I love you all, and may God bless you!

Preface

I wish to use this preface to set the stage for my readers as they get ready to read this book. Believers are at war with the kingdom of darkness. It is not, however, a war in which machines guns and bombers are used; it is, rather, a spiritual warfare in which spiritual weapons are used. There is war because the spiritual forces of darkness do not want the Kingdom of God to reign in the hearts of God's people. So, they weary God's children with attacks and temptations, hoping that they will yield to pressure. It cannot be overemphasized that Satan and his kingdom have some heinous agenda on the earth to oppose all that God stands for—and you are in the middle of that conflict!

Every day, people are feeling the effects of evil forces and yet, they don't know how to combat these evil forces. The spiritual war could be intense as to make even believers to wonder if actually there are redeemed by the Blood of Jesus Christ. Actually, you're primarily targeted by the enemy because you are redeemed—although there are other reasons why someone may be attacked (e.g. the anointing that you carry in you that you may not know about). You are now a threat to the kingdom of darkness, so the opposition against you increases.

Therefore, it is not enough for the believer to be redeemed. The believer should know how to fight with his/her spiritual weapons. He/she must be a warrior using his/her weapons to bind the forces of darkness, spoil their goods, pull down their strongholds, and cast down their wicked works. Once the believer has entered into this type of warfare, he/she can then claim back all what the devil has taken from him/her.

God has given us spiritual weapons of warfare to use in engaging the enemy in spiritual combats or conflicts. It is with these weapons that we can be able to recover our stolen blessings. God's weapons of warfare are unimaginably powerful!

This book, *The Warrior's Weapons,* takes you on a 21-day prayer program. Each chapter is divided into two parts: Part 1 and Part 2. It has a teaching component in Part 1 and a prayer session in Part 2. While the teaching component presents reflections aimed at acquiring spiritual knowledge on how to use the spiritual weapons, the prayer component presents warfare prayers devised to enable you to overtake the enemy with God's weapons. It has some inspiring stories to motivate you to expect your own testimonies. The book comes as a series.

This prayer manual will help you develop a proactive strategy to overthrow the enemy's agenda against your life. So prepare yourself for spiritual battles as God's warrior. I pray that this book brings out the warrior in you!

God bless you!

Uwakwe C. Chukwu
Simpsonville, South Carolina, USA
June, 2019

Introduction

"For the weapons of our warfare are not carnal, but mighty through God to the pulling down of strongholds."
2 Corinthians 10:4.

[Other suggested Bible passages to read:
Ephesians 6:10-11, I Peter 5:8-9, 2 Corinthians 10:3-6,
Ephesians 6:14-18, 2 Chronicles 20:5-30, Mark 16:17-18,
Luke 10:17-20, 2 Kings 1:9-15, Exodus 10:22-23].

Never in the history of mankind has there been an era of war like ours. We could smell war in the air. While the media reminds us of physical wars, the struggles we go through every day remind us of spiritual wars. In a sense, it seems that there is an outbreak of demonic hostilities. Evidence abounds that supports the perception that more people are under bondage in this age than in any other period of human civilization. Many destinies are imprisoned and many more people, unfortunately, are seeking solutions in the wrong places. Families are going through herculean problems that defy solutions. The horror we see in our time ratifies the preaching that the devil is indeed all out to fight mankind. We fail to live in reality when we deny the reality of a raging spiritual war. Dear child of God, listen: we are all living in a war zone!

Now that we know that we are at war, so what? What are we going to do about it? I suggest that, because this is a war, we must begin to think militarily— and, perhaps, even more offensively. We must have some weapons of warfare. We must take stock of our weapons and how we can best use them to stop the enemy and his forces. It wouldn't do us much good to have a tank or a sophisticated aircraft armed with electronic weaponry at our disposal if we do not know how to use them. We would be as helpless as a little boy trying to fly a jet fighter!

Similarly, if we are to survive in these trying times in which we live, it is imperative that we learn about these weapons of warfare and use them effectively against the devil and his companions because we have entered the time period referred to in the Bible: *"For the devil has come down to you with great wrath, because he knows that his time is short!"* (Revelation 12:12).

Pause a little bit before you read **2 Corinthians 10: 3-4.** Read it slowly. It says, *"For though we walk in the flesh, we do not war according to the flesh. For the weapons of our warfare are not carnal but mighty in God for pulling down strongholds."* Three things overtly stand out in this Scripture: (1) There is warfare underway, (2) It involves us, and (3) We have specific weapons with which to fight this war. My dear, we cannot afford to be aloof.

We are in a spiritual war and it is a critical war. It is a fight to kill! It behooves *"a good soldier of Jesus Christ"* to take up his spiritual weapons (**2 Timothy 2:3**). Our spiritual weapons are *"not carnal but mighty through God for the pulling down of strongholds"* (**2 Corinthians 10:4, KJV**). We don't have to merely wound the enemies; rather, we should utterly destroy them with our spiritual weapons. Therefore, we ought to take our stand against the devil and his kingdom with our weapons. Jesus Christ is saying to His soldiers, *"Put on the whole armor of God, so that you may be able to stand against the wiles of the devil"* (Ephesians 6:11). Only soldiers put on armor, don't they? That's what Jesus expects from His soldiers. No soldier goes to battle weaponless and without armor. The true Church is God's Army. God has reserved unique weapons for a special squad in His army. This may surprise you, but it is true: In putting on our full armor of God and wielding our weapons, we become true allies of the Lord Jesus Christ in His determination to *"destroy the works of the devil"* (1 John 3:8). Since this is a war, the enemies also come to fight against us with their own weapons. The good news is that we have God's promise in **Isaiah 54:17** saying that, *"No weapon that is fashioned against [us] shall prosper"*

Once we understand that we are warriors engaged in a spiritual battle, then the first question that each and every one of us may want to ask is: *"Where are my armor and my weapons?"* The answer to this question begins with a correct understanding of the definition and purpose of an armor and a weapon. Thus:

> *A weapon may be defined as any device you can use that destroys your enemy's ability to wage war against you! With this definition in mind, a spiritual weapon is, therefore, simply defined as any device or instrument that a warring child of God can use to effectively destroy Satan's ability to wage war against him or her! Spiritual weapons are spiritual offensive weapons.*

> *An Armor is a metal covering formerly worn by soldiers or warriors to protect the body in time of battle. With this definition in mind, the armor of God is the warrior's uniform that we wear spiritually in order to defend ourselves when Satan attacks us. Armor is a spiritual shield that God has given to every Christian. This is a spiritual defensive weapon.*

No soldier goes to battle without carrying his weapons. Also, no good soldier goes to war carrying only one weapon; rather, he wears his armor and carries many weapons. One of the tragedies of our time is that so many Christians have dropped their weapons and armors.

Notice that Paul, in **2 Corinthians 10:4,** used the plural form of weapon (i.e., weapons), meaning that there is more than just one weapon. On the other side, the devil also has many weapons as evidenced by Paul's use of the word "wiles" (in the plural form) — *"Put on the whole armor of God, so that you may be able to stand against the wiles of the devil"* **(1 Peter 5:8).**

The numbers of weapons in God's armory are unlimited. We need the full armor of God and all the weapons in our arsenal with which we can wage war against the evil ones. Each piece of armor has a purpose and is designed for our protection and covering. Each of the weapons carries the power of the Lord God Almighty. These weapons are used to fight the enemy (spiritual offensive weapons) as well as to protect us from the attacks of the enemy (spiritual defensive weapons). I cannot help but think of God's "Weapons Room" fully-equipped and reserved for those who are determined to fight against their spiritual enemy.

In my years of ministry, I have seen Christians wounded and defeated. I have seen many Christians who have dropped out of the Christian journey. Many more have been carried away or drowned in the sea of worldliness. This is not supposed to be the case. A Christian is supposed to remain in the race! One of the reasons why this is happening is that most Christians do not really resist the enemy—the devil and his kingdom of darkness. This is connected to the fact that most Christians do not know how to fight spiritual warfare, not to talk of knowing how to map out battle strategies using God's armor and weapons to stop the advancing enemy. It is a disturbing trend in the Body of Christ!

I preach and teach spiritual warfare. How would my teachings travel far and wide to benefit more people who need help with spiritual engagements? I find the answer as my mind subtly tells me: "Put your teachings into books." On this note, I am presenting this book, *"The Warrior's Weapons"* to the Body of Christ. As you will discover yourself, this book is a prayer manual put together to bring out the fire of God in you. Use it for your warfare prayer! Warfare requires a good offense, a good defense, and wise effective intelligence. The knowledge you would obtain from this book will not only equip you with tactful warfare strategies, but would help you to know your enemy and his schemes, know your weapons, and also have a deeper knowledge of God's power unto your deliverance. Jesus Christ is your Commander!

In this book, we shall be discussing some strategic weapons in our spiritual arsenal and how they are to be used against the kingdom of darkness. I am far from saying that there are as many weapons in God's weapon room as discussed in this book. Certainly, there is a staggering number of weapons in God's weapon room— some of which I am familiar with but could not feature in this book because of space. Nevertheless, with certainty, I am persuaded that the ones presented in this book are indeed weapons. You will agree with me that these are powerful weapons of warfare as you start using them in your prayers. In fact, this book, itself, is a weapon of warfare! I prayed for that!

This book will help you attain a level of mastery in spiritual warfare that keeps you in the battle frontline. Experienced deliverance ministers and experts in spiritual warfare are not strangers to the unique and diverse weapons that God has given to the Church. The Psalmist must be a proven warlord as his hands are taught to war and fingers are taught to fight (Psalm 144:1).

As we are gradually coming to the end of this introductory chapter, I wish to make it clear that we shall not defeat the devil by reasoning with him, and not even by negotiating with him. We defeat the devil by putting on our full armor of God and by using the weapons of our warfare that are mighty through God. We must not take a defensive posture in the spiritual operation. We must have the aggressiveness of the military. We are not going to retreat.

Rather, with effrontery, we are going to lambast the devil's territory and free those in bondage. Confront the strongman sitting over your family's destiny with your spiritual weapons. Reclaim your family members and loved ones for the Kingdom of Heaven!

Now is the time for you to storm the gates of hell, overcome the strongman, and take the spoils away from him with your spiritual weapons. You would be required to go through 21 days of fasting and prayers with this book using the prayer structure presented in Table 1. This prayer program may be done as an individual or together as a family, prayer group, Church or Ministry.

TABLE 1

A 21 – DAY PRAYER PROGRAM USING THIS BOOK

DAY	CHAPTER TO STUDY AND PRAY WITH	FASTING PERIOD
Day 1	Introduction	12:00am - 1:0pm
Day 2	Chapter 1: The Blood of Jesus Christ (Part 1)	
Day 3	Chapter 1: The Blood of Jesus Christ (Part 2)	
Day 4	Chapter 2: The Holy Eucharist (1) (Part 1)	
Day 5	Chapter 2: The Holy Eucharist (1) (Part 2)	
Day 6	Chapter 3: The Holy Eucharist (2) (Part 1)	
Day 7	Chapter 3: The Holy Eucharist (2) (Part 2)	
Day 8	Chapter 4: The Power of Sacrifice (Part 1)	12:00am - 3:00pm
Day 9	Chapter 4: The Power of Sacrifice (Part 2)	
Day 10	Chapter 5: The Name of Jesus Christ (Part 1)	
Day 11	Chapter 5: The Name of Jesus Christ (Part 2)	
Day 12	Chapter 6: The Word of God (Part 1)	
Day 13	Chapter 6: The Word of God (Part 2)	
Day 14	Chapter 7: The Fire of God (Part 1)	
Day 15	Chapter 7: The Fire of God (Part 2)	
Day 16	Chapter 8: The Power of the Holy Spirit (Part 1)	
Day 17	Chapter 8: The Power of the Holy Spirit (Part 2)	
Day 18	Chapter 9: Prayer and Fasting (Part 1)	
Day 19	Chapter 9: Prayer and Fasting (Part 2)	12:00am - 6:00pm
Day 20	Chapter 10: The Angels of Angels (Part 1)	
Day 21	Chapter 10: The Angels of Angels (Part 2)	

Having gone through this chapter and seeing the need to think militarily, would you consider yourself a *"good soldier of Christ Jesus"* (2 Timothy 2:3)? I want to introduce you to a prayer for the soldiers of Christ. This prayer is called the *"Warrior's Prayer."* Yes, a "Warrior's Prayer" because you are a "warrior" for Christ. It is our first prayer in this book—and, who knows, it could be your daily prayer! You will be invited daily to make this prayer during each day's prayer in the course of the 21 days prayer program presented in this book.

The Warrior's Prayer

"Heavenly Father,
Your warrior prepares for battle.
Today I claim victory over Satan
By putting on the whole armor of God!
"I put on the Girdle of Truth!
May I stand firm in the truth of Your Word
So I will not be a victim of Satan's lies.
"I put on the Breastplate of Righteousness!
May it guard my heart from evil
So I will remain pure and holy,
Protected under the Most Precious Blood of Jesus Christ.
"I put on the Shoes of Peace!
May I stand firm in the Good News of the Gospel
So Your peace will shine
Through me and be a light to all I encounter.
"I take the Shield of Faith!
May I be ready for Satan's fiery darts of doubt,
denial, and deceit
So I will not be vulnerable to a spiritual defeat.
"I put on the Helmet of Salvation!
May I keep my mind focused on You
So Satan will not have a stronghold on my thoughts.

"I take the Sword of the Spirit!
May the two-edged sword of Your Word be ready in my hands
So I can expose the tempting words of Satan.
By faith, your warrior has put on the whole armor of God!
I am prepared to live this day in spiritual victory.
Amen!"

—Unknown Author

Spiritual communion with Christ is also an integral part of this prayer exercise. Spiritual communion is a practice of desiring union with Jesus Christ in the Holy Eucharist. Although this prayer may be used to prepare our hearts before receiving the Holy Communion, it is also used by individuals who cannot receive Communion. Therefore, we shall be making the prayer of *"The Act of Spiritual Communion"* during the 21 days prayer program. However, you can make this prayer from anywhere you might happen to be, at any time, day or night. It is a simple and powerful prayer to recharge your spirit and conquer the enemies! Therefore, brethren, it behooves you to use this prayer daily!

The Act of Spiritual Communion

"My Jesus, I believe that You are present in the
Most Holy Sacrament.
I love You above all things, and I desire to receive
You into my soul.
Since I cannot at this moment receive You sacramentally,
come at least spiritually into my heart.
I embrace You as if You were already there
and unite myself wholly to You.
Never permit me to be separated from You.
Amen!"

–St. Alphonsus Liguori

NOTE:

- This book is written for all of you who acknowledge that there is a battle and who seek a way out. And if you dismiss the notion of spiritual warfare, then I suggest you ask God in prayer to enlighten you. Keep this book handy for when this battle is revealed to you, you will find it a gold in your hand.

- If you are a Catholic, you are encouraged to consider receiving the Sacraments of reconciliation (confession) and Holy Communion either during or before you begin praying using this book.

DAY 1 - Warfare Prayers

1. Praise and worship God as the Holy Spirit leads you.

2. Pray and ask God for the forgiveness of your sins using **Psalm 51.**

3. Put on the full armor of God by praying *"The Warrior's Prayer"* (see the prayer as above).

4. Pray *"The Act of Spiritual Communion"* prayer (see the prayer as above).

5. Pray **Psalm 35** for deliverance from the spiritual enemies.

6. Pray and ask God to make you armed and dangerous as you go through this 21 days of spiritual battle. In the name of Jesus Christ, I confess that:
    a. I am covered with the Most Precious Blood of Jesus Christ. Therefore, no fiery arrow of the enemy shall get into me;
    b. The testimonies that I am getting through this prayer is covered with the Most Precious Blood of Jesus Christ. Therefore, every plot to stop my testimonies is intercepted and rendered impotent by the Blood of Jesus Christ.

7. I am fully armed and dangerous because I am carrying:

a. The Word of God as the piercing sword of the Spirit (**Ephesians 6:17**);

b. The Word of God in my *"mouth to tear up and to knock down, to destroy and to overthrow"* (**Jeremiah 1: 10**);

c. God's *"flames of fire"* (**Hebrews 1:7**);

d. The anointing of victory as I get into the battlefields with praise like King Jehoshaphat (**2 Chronicles 20:5-30**);

e. A *"tongue [that] is like a sharp razor"* (**Psalm 52:2**);

f. A tongue like *"sharp swords"* (**Psalm 57:4**);

g. The anointing that destroys every yoke;

h. The power of the Holy Spirit moving me to make great exploits (**Daniel 11:32**);

i. The garment of prayer that destroys every stubborn problem as I pray;

j. The presence of God's Angels ever-ready to disgrace every demon spirit on a mission to arrest me;

k. The faith that subdues kingdoms, stops the mouths of lions, quenches the violence of fire, and turns to flight all foreign armies (**Hebrews 11:33-34**);

l. The faith in God that overcomes the world (**1 John 5:4**);

m. The name of Jesus Christ that forces every enemy to bow (**Philippians 2:10**);

n. The love of Christ that takes away all that is evil;

o. The testimony of Christ that overcomes the enemy (**Revelation 12:11**);

p. The glory of Jesus Christ as I receive Him in the Eucharist;

q. Spiritual knowledge so that I cannot be *"outwitted by Satan"* (**2 Corinthians 2:11**);

r. The authority to trample on serpents and scorpions, and over all the power of the enemy, so that nothing shall by any means hurt me (**Luke 10:19**);

s. The authority to *"cast out demons"*, in the name of Jesus Christ (**Mark 16:17**);

t. The authority of God Almighty to crush the head of the

serpent **(Genesis 3:15)**;

u. The Power of God in my mouth. With it, I command every mountain to *"Be taken up and thrown into the sea"* **(Mark 11:23)**;

v. The Lord's *"battle-ax and weapons of war"* for breaking into pieces every barrier set up by the enemies against me **(Jeremiah 51:20)**;

w. The *"hands for war"* **(Psalm 144:1)**;

x. The garment of a *"conqueror through"* Christ **(Romans 8:37)**;

y. The feet that *"thresh the mountains and ... make the hills like chaff"* **(Isaiah 41:15)**;

z. The promise of God that *"No weapon formed against [me] shall prosper, and every tongue which rises against [me] in judgment [I] shall condemn"* **(Romans 8:37)**.

8. Begin to thank the Lord Jesus Christ for making you His battle ax **(Jeremiah 51:20)**. I thank You, Lord Jesus Christ:

a. For equipping me with Your full armor and weapons of warfare;

b. For training me to use my armor and weapons of warfare;

c. For always keeping Your promises;

9. Sing songs of Thanksgiving to the Lord Jesus Christ.

10. I cover this prayer with the Most Precious Blood of Jesus Christ (7 times).

Chapter 1

The Blood of Jesus Christ

"But they have conquered him by the blood of the Lamb and by the word of their testimony"

(Revelation 12:11)

[Other suggested Bible passages to read:
Mark 14:22-24, Matthew 26:26–28, Leviticus 17:11, John 6:53–56,
Hebrews 9:14, Colossians 1:20, Acts 20:28, Hebrews 9:22, 1 John 1:7,
Hebrews 10:19, Revelation 1:5, Romans 3:24-25, 1 Peter 1:18-19, John
6:55-59, 1 Corinthians 11:24-30, Isaiah 53:5, Exodus 12:13, Hebrews
13:20-21, Hebrews 12:24, Zechariah 9:11, Ephesians 1:7].

DAY 2 - Part 1: Reflection

Jesus Christ died to reconcile us all with God on the foundation of His Most Precious Blood. There is eternal life in the Blood of Jesus Christ; that life is the very Life of God Himself. His Blood is His Life, and this Life is inputted into us as we drink His Precious Blood **(John 6:56)**. The miracle of our salvation took place through the Precious Blood of Jesus Christ. A few drops of His Blood renewed the whole world, for all men, and at all time. We see the river of mercy flowing as the Blood and Water flow from His pierced sacred side **(John 19:34)**. You see, the Blood of Jesus Christ is absolutely the most precious thing that God has offered us. More so, the greatest expression of God's love toward us is the Blood of Jesus.

The Blood of Jesus Christ has redeeming power (**Ephesians 1:7; Colossians 1:14**), has justifying power (**Hebrews 13: 12**), has propitiating power (**Romans 3:25**), has purchasing power (**I Peter 1:18-19, Acts 20:28, Revelation 5:9**), has pacifying power (**Colossians 1 :20**), has cleansing power (**I John 1:7**), has destroying power (**Hebrews 2: 14**), has protecting power (**Exodus 12:13, Hebrews 9:14**), has Life-giving power (**John 6:53**), and also has an overcoming power that totally destroys the devil and all his works, including his stings of death (**Revelation 12: 11**). As can be seen, in the Blood of Jesus, we find a variety of Divine benefits.

When you go to the doctors, one of the things that they do as part of their evaluation is to draw your blood because they want to see what is in it. Your blood reveals your life! As the Scripture says, *"the life of the flesh is in the blood"* (**Leviticus 17:11**). So the Blood of Jesus Christ reveals the very Life of God!

More so, a sample of your blood reveals everything in your life and about your life. It contains everything about you, including the sickness that is troubling your life. Your blood is your chemistry!

Likewise, a sample of the Blood of Jesus Christ contains the Chemistry of His Divine Blood (or Divine Nature): Forgiveness, Protection, Deliverance, Healing, Life, Righteousness, and the list continues without end! You can receive healing through the Blood from His stripes (**Isaiah 53:5**). You can protect your household with His Blood like the people of Israel, while in Egypt, applying the animal blood for protection from destructive plague (**Exodus 12:13**). You can cover your entire household with the Blood of Jesus Christ (**Job 1:5**). You can also apply Christ's Blood on all your belongings. Whatever you apply the Blood of Jesus Christon assumes the seal of Christ— and Satan cannot touch it. Know this: There is power in the Blood of Jesus Christ!

The other day, the angel of death did not kill any of the Israelite's firstborn because he saw some blood applied to the doorposts and lintels of their houses **(Exodus 12:7)**. If the blood of an animal would keep away an angel of death, would the Blood of Jesus Christ not perfectly protect you from the demonic forces? It stands to reason that the Blood of Jesus Christ would do better things than the blood of animals.

Unfortunately, many Christians are drowning in the sea of troubles simply because they do not know how powerful the Blood of Jesus Christ is. Do you know the overwhelming power that is in the Blood of Jesus Christ? If you do, you will do great exploits **(Daniel 11:32)**. We are entitled to use the Blood of Jesus Christ to go on the offensive against any adversity that may come our way from the kingdom of darkness.

Blood is so important to God that it is mentioned in the Bible about 700 times. David referred to the *"incorruptible"* Blood **(Psalm 16:10 and confirmed in Acts 2:27, 31)**. Peter spoke of the *"precious"* Blood **(I Peter 1:18-19)**, and John wrote of the *"overcoming"* power of the Blood **(Revelation 12:11)**. If you are in Christ, His *"incorruptible"*, *"precious"*, and *"overcoming"* Blood is in your DNA!

I think of the Bible as having invisible veins in its verses with the Blood of Jesus Christ running through it in every heartbeat of God! The Blood of Jesus Christ is at the very core of Christianity. It is the foundation of our Christian faith. For this reason, critics thought it was a "bloody religion" because of all the frequent mention of blood in the Bible, and, ultimately, with the bloody death of its Cornerstone, Jesus Christ, on the Cross. What is it about the Blood of Jesus Christ? All that God has in stock for our victorious living!

We are going to pay attention to the **Revelation 12** account on the Blood of Jesus Christ because it highlights that it was the weapon that defeated the archenemy of man, the devil. The Blood of Jesus Christ has provided everything we need to live a life of victory. That's how powerful the blood is! **Revelation 12:3-4** tells us of *"an enormous red dragon with seven heads and ten horns and seven crowns on its heads. Its tail swept a third of the stars out of the sky and flung them to the earth."* Its saliva was like a river **(Revelation 12:15)**.

Revelation 12:9 calls this great dragon, the *"ancient serpent, who is called the devil and Satan."* He makes war with mankind but selectively and furiously attacking *"those who keep the commandments of God and hold the testimony of Jesus"* **(Revelation 12:17)**. No wonder the Scripture lamented saying in **Revelation 12:12**, *"But woe to the earth and the sea, for the devil has come down to you with great wrath."* We were told that *"the great dragon was thrown down...he was thrown down to the earth, and his angels were thrown down with him"* **(Revelation 12:9)**.

The *"ancient serpent"* was defeated but not without a war—*"And war broke out in heaven; Michael and his angels fought against the dragon. The dragon and his angels fought back"* **(Revelation 12:7)**. How did heaven defeat or overcome the devil in their midst? **Revelation 12:11** gives the secret of their weapon of warfare as recorded in **Revelation 12:11**—*"But they have conquered him by the Blood of the Lamb and by the word of their testimony."*

Revelation 12:11 registers an undeniable fact that the Blood of Jesus Christ is an extremely powerful force in the believer's repertoire of spiritual weapons. It is our greatest weapon against the enemy! The devil cannot stand the power of the Blood of Jesus Christ. There's deliverance power in His Blood.

Therefore, wisdom demands that we place ourselves, family, and possessions on the Altar of the Blood of Jesus every day—for by doing so, even the most wicked tyrant spirits, cannot come near us. We ought to be covering ourselves and all that belong to us every day with the Blood of Jesus Christ for protection from demonic spirits.

I enjoy seeing demons writhe in anguish and flee as I plead the Blood of Jesus Christ during deliverance sessions. When we start declaring the Blood of Jesus Christ, we introduce the very life and Power of God into our midst. Nothing compares to the Power of the Blood of Jesus.

Now that you know that there's great power of protection in the Blood of Jesus Christ, why not consider walking completely around your entire property pleading the Blood of Jesus Christ? By doing this, a line of Jesus' Blood is marked on the ground, tracing your pathway. It is like drawing a Bloodline on the ground with the Blood of Jesus Christ. In fact, we may rightly call this method of prayer "drawing the Bloodline." The Bloodline becomes an invisible electric fence of protection erected around you, your household, your estate, and all that you have on every side. You may not see it but it is there!

I once came across the testimony of a poultry owner who employed the Bloodline to protect his birds from dying mysteriously. This farmer discovered that his birds were dying without any known cause. It was clear to him that he would soon be out of business if the situation continues. After trying everything to arrest the situation without success, he got up one night and walked around his entire property, "drawing the Bloodline."

When he woke up the next day, he discovered that no bird died. To his great surprise, he found a dead wolf lying about two feet past the path of the Bloodline that he made the day before. It is evidently clear that the wolf had crossed over the Bloodline and got spiritually electrocuted by the Power in Blood of Jesus Christ. Since after this event, the farmer never had any other mysterious death of his birds.

Are you surprised that the wolf died? If you are surprised, then my question is: "why?" Are you surprised when you see birds electrocuted on electric wires? Bloodline pretty does the same when evil elements venture to come near. Bloodline is like a naked wire that carries killer voltages! How can a demonic entity rest on a naked wire and survive it? Touching such a naked wire is to accept a death sentence! Would you like your body to be electrocuting witchcraft spirits or other demonic spirits that are attempting to attack you? The answer is simple: Apply the Bloodline over your life or circle of operations. You become a "Danger Zone" for the enemy when you are encircled by the Bloodline.

I once had a spiritual battle in which I was fighting a python spirit. Upon seeing that the battle was tough, the spirit flew into the air with a terrific speed and headed to my family to go and attack them. Then I heard the voice of the Angel of God saying to me in a loud voice, *"It is heading to South Carolina to attack your family: Pray! Pray!! Pray!!!"* Then only immediately I started praying did I see a giant wall that appeared in the air preventing the spirit from heading to attack my family. That spiritual wall is the manifestation of the Bloodline. You need it activated in your life!

Would you consider today to draw a Bloodline over all that God has given to you? The blood on the doorpost of the Israelites was a bloodline **(Exodus 12:13)**. It saved the lives of their firstborns **(Exodus 12:7)**. If you apply Christ's Bloodline over your life and your loved ones, the devil will honor the badge of warning sign over your dominion: *"Do not touch my anointed ones; do my prophets no harm"* **(Psalm 105:15)**. The Bloodline speaks for you. It can save you from accident and pestilence and can protect your belongings from disaster. That is how powerful it is!

Apply it to someone hit with a life-threatening illness or disease. What about your loved ones who are alcoholics or drug addicts and seem not to break free from it in spite of efforts made to be free? Apply it! Do you know of someone who is under severe demonic attack as a result of engaging in some type of occult activity? Apply it! Perhaps you may know someone else who is severely depressed and they are seriously contemplating suicide. Don't fail to apply the Bloodline.

As we are coming to the end of this chapter, I would wish to highlight the importance of the Blood of Jesus Christ as *"the Blood of the eternal covenant"* (Hebrews 13: 20). Understanding this is very important in warfare because, in spiritual battles, it is your covenant that fights for you! You are set free by the covenant that is covering your life. Ponder on this Scripture: *"As for you also, because of the blood of my covenant with you, I will set your prisoners free from the waterless pit"* (Zechariah 9:11).

Zechariah 9:11 simply tells us that our covenant stands for us in the times of danger. In the same way, the covenant with the Blood of Jesus Christ speaks for you if you have a covenant relationship with the Living God, and walk in that covenant. This means that the Blood of Jesus speaks Life into your life where the devil has spoken otherwise. Covenant is powerful! It is very powerful, and the devil knows! Our covenant with the Blood of Jesus Christ is the devil's headache! The kingdom of darkness knows that they cannot have their way to attack God's people when God's people are under the covering of the Blood of Jesus Christ.

David anchored on his covenant with God before going to fight Goliath. We see this covenant displayed as David says to Goliath: *"You come to me with sword and spear and javelin; but I come to you in the name of the LORD of hosts, the God of the armies of Israel"* (1 Samuel 17:45). Even Goliath himself also came to fight David based on his own covenant with the god of the Philistines— and that was why Goliath *"cursed David by his gods"* (1 Samuel 17:43). That historical war was actually a conflict of covenants.

We usually make the mistake to think that it was David's stone that killed Goliath: No, it was the power of God propelling the stone.

It was David's covenant with God that moved the power of God into the battle scene. The victory came not because David was a Jew but because he walked in his covenant relationship with the Living God. God proved Himself *"a man of war"* when David walked on the path of covenant with God **(Exodus 15:3, KJV)**. We should always remember that Israel was in a covenant with God but not all of them were walking in that covenant. David did!

Through a covenant with the Blood of Jesus Christ, God equipped the Church to confront her spiritual enemies. Regrettably, many people of God walk defeated in spiritual battles because they do not walk in their covenant relationship with God. It is not answering a Christian that gives you victory over the enemy; rather, it is having a covenant relationship with the Living God, and through Christ, walking in that covenant.

Imagine this small boy, David, in a battlefield with only one weapon: his covenant with God. If you were there, would you not pity him? Yet, his victory over Goliath speaks eloquently of the power of covenant and of walking in it. Although *"covenant"* as a weapon of warfare is not discussed as a chapter in this book, it is a weapon! [Don't forget that in the Introductory Chapter of this book, it was mentioned that there are numerous weapons of warfare not discussed in this book because of the limitation of space].

LET US PRAY!

1. Reflect on how this reflection on *"The Blood of Jesus Christ"* ministers to you.

2. Pray and ask God for the forgiveness of your sins using **Psalm 51.**

3. Put on the full armor of God by praying *"The Warrior's Prayer"* (see page 18).

4. Pray *"The Act of Spiritual Communion"* prayer (see page 19)

5. Pray **Psalm 35** for deliverance.

6. Place your hands on the various parts of your body and pray aggressively like this: *"I invoke the power in the Blood of Jesus Christ over my stomach, navel, kidney, liver, intestine, blood, eyes, head, heart, lungs (continue to do so over every part of your body that the enemy is attacking)."*

7. I call upon the Blood of Jesus Christ to destroy everything that sabotages my testimonies and my relationship with God —in the name of Jesus Christ.

8. I call upon the Blood of Jesus Christ to disconnect my life from failure at the edge of breakthroughs, in the name of Jesus Christ.

9. Lord Jesus, grant me Divine Immunity by the anti-viral effect of Your Most Precious Blood - I pray in the name of Jesus Christ.

10. By the Blood of Jesus Christ, I dismantle every evil weapon that is fashioned against me, in the name of Jesus Christ.

11. In the name of Jesus Christ, I now plead the Blood of Jesus over ..... *(pick from the following list).*

- My children *(name them)*
- My spouse
- My marriage
- My testimonies
- Going out and coming in
- Every inch of soul
- Every inch of my spirit
- Every inch of my body
- Every inch of my entire life
- My conscious mind
- My subconscious mind
- My conscience
- My emotions
- My thoughts
- My motives
- My intuition
- My intellect
- My will
- My actions
- My character

- My business
- My commitments
- The land
- The air around me
- My foundation
- Everyone here
- My future
- My time

- My health
- My worship
- My calling
- My possessions
- My job
- My sleep
- My ways

12. Thank You Lord Jesus Christ for answering my prayers. I cover this prayer with the Most Precious Blood of Jesus Christ (7 times).

DAY 3 - Part 2: Warfare Prayers

Note:
- The Blood of Jesus Christ is the terror of demons and vanquisher of rebel spirits.

- Walking in the covenant relationship with the Blood of Jesus Christ, use the weapon of this Blood to break free from every bondage!

- At the end of each prayer point below that ends with "in the name of Jesus Christ," please proclaim "Amen!"

1. Something happens as we step out in faith and begin to sing songs that portray the Blood of Jesus Christ. Such songs are appreciative tributes to the sacrifice made by Jesus, giving His life to redeem our souls. Such songs cause terrible havoc to the kingdom of darkness. The following songs are suggested to get started....

   a. Sing the song with the Chorus: *"There is power, power, wonder-working power in the blood of the Lamb. There is power, power, wonder-working power in the precious blood of the Lamb"*.

b. *"Blood of Jesus, Blood of Jesus, Blood of Jesus, cover us"* (X3)
c. *"The Blood of Jesus set me free, from sin and sorrow, the Blood of Jesus set me free."*
d. Continue with other songs that portray the Blood of Jesus Christ.

2. *"In Him, we have redemption through His Blood, the forgiveness of our trespasses, according to the riches of His grace"* (**Ephesians 1:7**). Therefore, release the weight of your sin to the Lord Jesus Christ. Ask the Lord Jesus to cleanse you with His all-cleansing Blood. Use **Psalm 51** to ask God for the forgiveness of your sins.
    a. The Blood of Jesus Christ cleanses me from all sin (**1 John 1:7**);
    b. I use the Blood of Jesus to reverse every record of the past that the devil holds against me;
    c. The Blood of Jesus Christ destroys the power of sin and iniquity in my life (**Hebrews 10:17**).

3. Put on the full armor of God by praying *"The Warrior's Prayer"* (see page 18).

4. Pray *"The Act of Spiritual Communion"* prayer (see page 19).

5. I cover myself and my household, and the environment of this prayer with the Most Precious Blood of Jesus Christ (7 times).

6. In the name of Jesus Christ, I now immerse my body, my soul, my spirit, and my entire life into the Most Precious Blood of Jesus Christ. Make the following prayers "in the name of Jesus Christ":
    a. I now ask that the Blood of Jesus Christ keeps me and my household into the most perfect will of God for our lives;
    b. I now plead the Blood of Jesus Christ against any demonic spirit that may try to come against me or my loved ones in any way or form.

7. Satan, hear me: Neither you nor your demons are allowed to operate against this prayer, in the name of Jesus Christ.

8. As the Red Sea swallowed up the armies of Pharaoh, so I ask the Blood of Jesus Christ to swallow up every tyrant red dragon that is pursuing my destiny and that of my loved ones, in the name of Jesus Christ.

9. I am a "Danger Zone" for the enemy because I am covered with the Blood of Jesus Christ—I pray in the name of Jesus Christ.

10. According to **Exodus 12:13,** I cover every entry point to my house with the Blood of Jesus Christ, in the name of Jesus Christ.

11. I now plead the Blood of Jesus Christ against any accidents or natural catastrophes that may come against me or my loved ones, in the name of Jesus Christ. Make the following prayers *"in the name of Jesus Christ":*
    a. I now plead the Blood of Jesus against any diseases, viruses, or illnesses that are projected at me and my loved ones;
    b. I raise the Blood of Jesus against the kingdom of darkness, in the name of Jesus Christ;
    c. According to **Revelation 12:11,** my family and I have overcome the devil through the Blood of Jesus Christ.

12. Let the Blood of Jesus Christ purge out of my body every evil material that is deposited in my womb of life to prevent me from bearing fruits and producing blessings, righteousness, and peace—in the name of Jesus Christ.

13. I place the Bloodline between me/my family and demonic forces that are targeting us, in the name of Jesus Christ.
14. Let the Blood of Jesus Christ be transfused into my own Blood, in the name of Jesus Christ.

15. O you powers militating against my fulfillment and upliftment in life, the Blood of Jesus Christ is against you today, in the name of Jesus Christ.

16. Let the Blood of Jesus Christ destroy every devourer that is hiding in my foundation, in the name of Jesus Christ.

17. I command every satanic case-file that is opened against my life to be closed forever by the Blood of Jesus Christ—in the name of Jesus Christ.

18. I command every evil ancestral law that is programmed into my genes to be terminated now, in the name of Jesus Christ.

19. Lord Jesus Christ, let Your Blood become like liquid fire to destroy every witchcraft curse that are working against my life and the lives of my loved ones—in the name of Jesus Christ.

20. I am delivered from the power of Satan unto God through the Blood of Jesus Christ (**Acts 26:18**), in the name of Jesus Christ.

21. I immerse myself in the Blood of Jesus Christ, in the name of Jesus Christ. Make the following prayers *"in the name of Jesus Christ"*. I immerse in the Blood of Jesus:
    a. My five senses: Sight, hearing, smell, taste, and touch;
    b. My physical body: Physical appetites and entire body organs;

22. *"As for you also, because of the blood of my covenant with you, I will set your prisoners free from the waterless pit"* (Zechariah **9:11**). Make the following prayers *"in the name of Jesus Christ"*:
    a. I stand on **Zechariah 9:11** to claim my freedom from every form of satanic imprisonment;
    b. I am made perfect through the Blood of the Everlasting Covenant (**Hebrews 13:20-21**).

23. Begin to make the following confessions (releasing the Power of the Blood of Jesus Christ). Make the following prayers *"in the name of Jesus Christ"*:

   a. I sprinkle the Blood of Jesus Christ and receive multiplied grace and peace **(1 Peter 1:2)**;

   b. I have the boldness to enter into the presence of God through the Blood of Jesus Christ **(Hebrews 10:19)**;

   c. My conscience is purged from dead works to serve the living God through the Blood of Jesus Christ **(Hebrews 9:14)**;

   d. I receive full spiritual benefits of the New Covenant through the Blood of Jesus Christ **(Matthew 26:28)**;

   e. I have redemption through the Blood of Jesus Christ and I am redeemed from the power of evil **(Ephesians 1:7)**;

   f. I rebuke and cast out all spirits of torment and fear because I have peace through the Blood of Jesus Christ **(Colossians 1:20)**;

   g. I receive healing and health through the Blood of Jesus Christ **(1 Peter 2:24)**;

   h. I receive the provisions of Heaven through the Blood of Jesus Christ **(2 Corinthians 8:9)**;

   i. I receive deliverance through the Blood of Jesus Christ **(Isaiah 54:5)**;

   j. The Blood of Jesus Christ bears witness to my salvation **(1 John 5:8)**;

   k. The Blood of Jesus Christ gives me victory **(Hebrews 12:4)**;

   l. I rebuke and cast out all spirits of guilt, shame, and condemnation through the Blood of Jesus Christ;

   m. I receive the fullness of the Holy Spirit and the Anointing through the Blood of Jesus Christ;

   n. My heart is sprinkled clean from an evil conscience with the Blood of Jesus Christ. **(Hebrews 10:22)**;

   o. I rebuke Satan and I remind him that he is defeated by the Blood of Jesus Christ **(Revelation 12:10)**;

   p. My entire being is now being washed clean with the Blood of Jesus Christ;

q. I overcome, by the Blood of Jesus Christ, every evil opposition that is approaching me and my loved ones;

r. Because of the Blood of Jesus Christ, I am free from eating from the table of the devil;

s. I confess that I am living my life inside the Blood of Jesus Christ;

t. I confess that my life is propelled by the Blood of Jesus Christ;

u. I am sanctified and set apart for God's purpose by the Blood of Jesus Christ;

v. I have divine life in me because the Blood of Jesus Christ flows through me;

w. Let the Blood of Jesus Christ speak against every evil altar raising their voice of condemnation and accusations against me and my loved ones:

    i. That condemnation shall not stand (John 8:10-11);

    ii. That accusation shall not stand (Romans 8:1);

    iii. I rebuke and cast out all spirits of slander (Matthew 12:10);

    iv. I silence the voice of evil spirits instigating suspicion, malice, persecution, and false accusations against me and my loved ones (Acts 16:19-40);

    v. The Blood of Jesus Christ speaks a better Word than the blood of demonic sacrifices speaking against me and my loved ones (Hebrews 12:24).

x. I place under the Blood of Jesus Christ everything in my life that may be troubled: fears, anxiety, sickness, confusion, brokenness, anger, and worry—and I leave them there at the foot of the Cross of Jesus Christ on Calvary;

y. By The Blood of Jesus Christ, I take authority over Satan and his principalities that oppress my family;

z. Nothing shall affect me or my family that does not first get screened through the Blood of Jesus Christ. Pray for screening through the Blood of Jesus Christ:

    i. Everything coming from:

- The enemy to me is screened by the Blood of Jesus Christ;
- The natural world to me is screened by the Blood of Jesus Christ.

    ii.   I let go of anything that cannot remain under the Blood of Jesus—any habits, any material things, any thoughts, any people;

   iii.   I choose to remain under the Blood of Jesus Christ and I claim all His provisions today for me and my family.

24. In the name of Jesus Christ, I now have full faith and belief that the Blood of Jesus Christ will now fully protect me against all of the things that I have just pled His Blood on through this prayer.

25. Thank You, Lord Jesus Christ, for permanently defeating the devil afflicting my life by the Power of Your Most Precious Blood!

    a.   Lord Jesus Christ, I thank You for setting me free by Your Precious Blood;

    b.   Sing songs of thanksgiving and praise to the Lord Jesus Christ.

26. I cover this prayer with the Most Precious Blood of Jesus Christ (7 times).

Chapter 2

The Holy Eucharist (1)

"And as they were eating, He took bread, and blessed, and broke it, and gave it to them, and said, 'Take; this is My Body.' And He took a cup, and when He had given thanks He gave it to them, and they all drank of it. And He said to them, 'This is My Blood of the covenant, which is poured out for many'"

(Mark 14:22-24).

[Other suggested Bible passages to read:
Mark 14:22-24, Matthew 26:26–28, Leviticus 17:11, John 6:53–56,
Hebrews 9:14, Colossians 1:20, Acts 20:28, Hebrews 9:22,
1 John 1:7, Hebrews 10:19].

DAY 4 - Part 1: Reflection

The Eucharist is the Body and Blood of Jesus Christ. It is a gift of Jesus to His Church at the Last Supper when He took bread, broke it, and gave it to His disciples, saying: *"Take and eat; this is My Body"* **(Matthew. 26:26).** The broken bread would then become His Body broken to make us whole again. It is definitely not a coincidence, but the fulfillment of a Divine plan that Christ's birth took place in the town of Bethlehem, meaning the "house of bread" and was laid in a manger, where food for animals would normally be placed.

In the same way, He took the cup, lifted it up, and said: *"Drink from it all of you. This is My Blood of the covenant which is poured out for many for the forgiveness of sins"* (Matthew 26:27–28). The wine would then become the Blood of Jesus Christ poured out for the remission of our sins. Upon consecration, the Eucharist becomes the Lord in Flesh and Blood. As we know, *"the life of the flesh is in the blood"* (Leviticus 17:11)—so Eternal Life is in the Blood of Jesus. This simply establishes the Eucharist as the apogee of spiritual life. It is the very Life of Christ! It is also the life that flows in the veins of the Body of Christ (the Church). Receiving Him in the Eucharistic Species (in the state of grace) is to receive the Body, Blood, Soul, and Divinity of Jesus Christ. The critical necessity for the Eucharist in the Church is obvious in Christ's command in His last days (not a suggestion, please) to *"Do this in remembrance of me"* (Luke 22:19). The gift of a father to his children in His last days must be taken seriously by his children. Am I right?

The Eucharist and the sacrifice of Christ on the Cross are one and inseparable. For Christ, the Eucharist is a serious business: *"Very truly I tell you, unless you eat the flesh of the Son of Man and drink His blood, you have no life in you...Whoever eats My flesh and drinks My Blood remains in me, and I in them"* (John 6:53–56, NIV). For Apostle Paul, the Eucharist is an *"indescribable gift!"* (2 Corinthians 9:15). For the Church, it is the broken Body that makes whole and the reason for coming together as one....But for the skeptics and unbelievers, it is *"foolishness"* (1 Corinthians 1:23)!

The Eucharist brings a direct assault on the devil and his forces! Eucharistic healing is not only a well-documented fact but a daily occurrence. I would jokingly ask you to imagine the Eucharist you swallowed swallowing up (or eating up) every sickness in you like when the rod of Moses became a snake and swallowed up the Egyptian magician's rods that were turned into snakes. Not to sound theoretical, let me share some experiences (out of many experiences that I have witnessed in ministry) to buttress the incredible power of the Eucharist. I hope these experiences removes every veil of doubt in the potency and trueness of the Eucharist.

During a certain deliverance session in which the Lord Jesus was Eucharistically exposed at the Altar, I encountered several demonic manifestations. One of such manifestations was a teenage girl who was possessed with a demon spirit. I commanded the spirit, *"In the name of Jesus Christ, tell me your name?"* To this, the spirit answered, *"My name is cancer."*

I then proceeded with deliverance prayers over her, but the spirit was stubborn. At a point, I noticed that the girl was intermittently gazing at the Eucharist enthroned at the Altar. Then, I got a Word of knowledge that she was seeing Something at the Altar. For this reason, I asked her, *"What are you seeing?"* Pointing her hand at the Altar, she responded, *"That thing there at the Altar."* I looked at the Altar again and all I could see was the white round Substance inside a monstrance—the Eucharist—but I knew she was seeing the Lord Jesus Himself.

Then she looked at me, as if afraid of something. I asked her, *"What is that?"* Then sobbing and trembling, she narrated, *"I saw that thing at the Altar radiating bright light. A man wearing sparkling white came out from it and touched me. Then, immediately, I saw black smoke leaving my body."*

I immediately knew it was Jesus that she saw proceeding from the Eucharist. I knew that she was healed as, in the Presence of Jesus, the black smoke was leaving her body. Out of curiosity, I asked in the Church if anyone knew the girl. Immediately, a man introduced himself to me as her father. *"What's wrong with your daughter?"* I asked. To this, he answered, *"She is battling with cancer...and she has had it for some years now."*

Most people would not believe that demons can play a role in physical illness, although it would be a mistake to give the devil credit for every sickness. In most cases, God may reveal to the deliverance minister the true cause of the sickness most times by vision or by the word of knowledge.

Undoubtedly, this girl saw Jesus Christ, the Healer **(Exodus 15:26)**. In the Eucharist, Jesus is a Healer: The same Jesus who is testified in the Bible as the wonder Worker who *"went about doing good and healing all who were oppressed by the devil"* **(Acts 10:38)**. The Body that was wounded for our healing is not a different Body in the Eucharist. He is still the same miracle Worker!

This girl had an encounter with the Power of Jesus in the Eucharist. Permit me to call Him the Eucharistic Jesus—that is, Jesus in the Eucharist—but not different from the Jesus in the womb of Mary. In the Eucharist, Jesus is still the Mighty Savior. Think about this: If He who the whole earth and the entire heavens could not contain would permit Himself to be contained in the little womb of a woman, would He not allow Himself to be contained in the little wafer of bread? In fact, because He was in Her womb, Mary may fittingly be described as the portal of the Eucharist. Scripture is already testifying to this fact when it says, *"The Lord has created a new thing on earth; a woman shall compass a man."* (Jeremiah 31:22).

We also carry Jesus within us when we receive Him in the Eucharist. We don't carry a "thing" when we receive Him in the Eucharist. He is not a "thing on the Altar" as the girl erroneously described in her story. He is but a "Him" or a "Being". He has never been a "thing" or a symbol of "Him". Rather, He has always been a "Him"—the Divine Substance, GOD! In the Eucharist, Christ is Himself present as God. It cannot be made clearer to us that Jesus gives Himself to us physically in the Eucharist. My dear friend, there in the Eucharist is The Real Presence of Christ! Was it not in the breaking of the bread (the Eucharistic meal) that the disciples discovered that He was the Lord Jesus **(Luke 24:35)**?

Although the appearance of bread and wine remains, the bread and wine truly become Jesus in Substance. Jesus, Himself, is really there present in Person in the Eucharist. We don't need to be convinced that the sun rises from the East. We know that this is an undeniable reality, don't we? So is the trueness of the Eucharist as Christ Himself! Jesus offers us every last bit of His whole Body in the Eucharist. I knew about this, not only from Scripture but by personal revelations and from experience in ministry.

What this girl saw and called "that thing" was the Mighty Jesus in His Being. Who else could have walked out from the Eucharist wearing bright light and walking towards her for a healing touch other than the One who said, *"I am the Lord who heals you"* (Exodus 15:26)? Oh lest I forget, He healed this girl! Is this not the fulfillment of the prophecy of Isaiah: *"And by His stripes, we are healed"* (Isaiah 53:5, NKJV)?

Can you imagine the healing anointing that is in the Eucharistic Jesus? When you receive the Eucharist, you eat God's healing Meal. It is the Meal that heals. So as you eat the Eucharist, you are taking in the very Life that is in Jesus Christ.

Think of what happens when you eat food in the natural: your body absorbs the nutrients that are in that food. So likewise, when you eat the Eucharist, your body begins to absorb the Life that is in the Blood of Jesus (don't forget **Leviticus 17:11** saying, *"The life of the flesh is in the blood")*. At the same time, while the food you eat is absorbed and becomes part of you, when you eat the Eucharist, however, you become part of Him.

In fact, in essence, through the Eucharist, the Life that is in Jesus Christ is transferred into us *"so that the Life of Jesus may also be made visible in our bodies"* (**2 Corinthians 4:10**). You see, when you receive the Eucharist in faith, you are receiving the benefits of Jesus' death and resurrection. Know it today that the Lord is present in the Eucharist to take away the afflictions of His people. He does make His people whole once again in the Eucharist. Such is the power of the Lord in the Eucharist!

I excuse this girl's improper description of the Eucharistic Jesus as "that thing" on the basis of ignorance. I believe that the bright light she saw is better described as the *"light ...brighter than the sun"* (Acts 26:13).

I came across a similar Eucharistic deliverance in an article written by Rev. Fr. Venatius Oforka[1]. Here is his story:

> *"During a deliverance session, a priest encountered a demon that had possessed a young girl for some years. The demon was tough and obstinate. He so resisted forfeiting the temple he had taken over that the priest was tempted to despair. The praying team was already becoming demoralized and discouraged. But then a thought came to him: 'Take him to the Eucharistic Jesus.' In the chapel, the Eucharistic Lord was brought out to stand as a great King reigning in the effulgence of glory and splendor from the monstrance on the altar.*
>
> *"The tide of events changed immediately. The demon shouted at the top of his voice and with great fright, 'Who is this! Who is this person?' For him, the Eucharist is "Who" and "Person," but for a nonspiritual eye it is "what" and "thing." We might be seeing a white round substance, but the demons see a Person, the Master in His glory. The demon saw the glory of God filling His temple and was dazed. He closed his eyes. He was now stuttering, 'Let me go. I don't want to see Him. Who brought me to His house? We don't like each other. Take me out of this place!'*
>
> *"'My God! What is he talking about?' the young priest thought to himself. 'Is he addressing the consecrated bread on the altar? But it was just this morning that I consecrated it at Mass. How could it be this powerful?' He reasoned myopically like the priest Zechariah, who ministered in the Holy of Holies*

---

1. https://catholicexchange.com/eucharistic-jesus-mighty-force-devil

but could still not believe the words of the archangel Gabriel...When he [the demon] saw that he had been cornered, he decided to engage the Master in a fight. His plan was to push Him down from the altar...

"*At first, the praying team tried to protect the Lord from being pushed down, but after some thoughts, the priest felt that He should be allowed to fight for Himself and asked the prayer ministers to let the demon do what he wished. The demon then rushed with a terrific speed and force toward the altar. But just an inch away from the altar, he stopped with an automatic halt, as if controlled electronically. He tried again and repeated the first experience. He drew back the third time, mustered all his strength and courage and tried again. This time he succeeded having a brush with the altar cloth. It was then that hell was let loose on him. The demon was rattling. He was thrown up high and dashed with a heavy thud on the hard floor and set into a bout of rolling, wriggling, and shouting until he begged to leave.*"

With such manifestations as described above, we just cannot but testify that in the Eucharist, Jesus is the invisible Reality reigning in the effulgence of His Majesty. ***"The Son of God [Who] was revealed for this purpose, to destroy the works of the devil"*** (1 John 3:8), is the same Man of war in the Eucharist routing demons and destroying their works.

LET US PRAY!
1. Reflect on how this reflection on "*The Holy Eucharist*" ministers to you.
   a. Reflect on **Proverbs 9:1-5** which says, "*I say, come, eat of my food, and drink of the wine I have mixed!*"
   b. Reflect on **Zechariah 9:15** which says, "*They shall drink blood like wine, till they are filled with it like libation bowls...*"
   c. Reflect on 1 **Kings 19:6-8** that says, "*After he [Elijah] ate and*

drank, he lay down again, but the angel of the LORD came back a second time, touched him, and ordered, "Get up and eat, else the journey will be too long for you!" He got up, ate and drank; then strengthened by that food, he walked forty days and forty nights to the mountain of God"

2. Pray and ask God for the forgiveness of your sins using **Psalm 51.**

3. Put on the full armor of God by praying *"The Warrior's Prayer"* (see page 18).

4. Pray *"The Act of Spiritual Communion"* prayer (see page 19).

5. Pray **Psalm 22** (a prayer for plea for deliverance from suffering and hostility).

6. *"Wheresoever the body shall be, there shall the eagles also be gathered together"* **(Matthew 24:28).** Make the following prayers *"in the name of Jesus Christ"*:
    a. Lord Jesus Christ, put in me a burning desire to joyfully gather with Your Saints wherever/whenever Your Body is dignified in the Eucharist;
    b. Lord Jesus Christ, grant me the grace to always keep my eyes fixed on You **(Hebrews 12:2);**
    c. Lord Jesus Christ, activate in me the love of the Eucharist;
    d. Lord Jesus Christ, as You revealed Yourself to Your disciples at the breaking of the bread, may You reveal Yourself to me in the Eucharist;
    e. Lord Jesus Christ, renew my desire to be totally Yours as You made Yourself totally mine in the Eucharist;
    f. May the Eucharist we celebrate guide us to the fullness of Christ's life;
    g. Lord Jesus Christ, I ask for Eucharistic miracles.

7. Thank You Lord Jesus Christ for answering my prayers. I cover this prayer with the Most Precious Blood of Jesus Christ (7 times).

DAY 5 - Part 2: Warfare Prayers

NOTE:

- The Holy Eucharist is a powerful defense against evil. Make the Holy Eucharist your greatest refuge. We have our being in Him **(Acts 17:28).**

- Examine yourself before you receive the Eucharist (Holy Communion). Before we partake, the Bible tells us to examine our hearts **(1 Corinthians 11:28-30).** Ask God for forgiveness in areas where you've missed the mark (strife, unforgiveness, jealousy, envy, hatred, covetousness, fear, worry, unbelief, etc.) Also, be sure you are not receiving the Eucharist just as a mere religious exercise, rather than accepting everything Jesus' sacrifice provides. Always receive the Holy Eucharist in a state of grace. If you have lost this grace through sin, please endeavor to first receive the Sacrament of Reconciliation before receiving the Eucharist.

- Thank God for the gift of the Eucharist. He made our redemption possible by His own Precious Blood and Life.

1. Honor the Lord by singing some Eucharistic songs, including songs that project the Most Precious Blood of Jesus Christ. The following songs are suggested to get started...
   a. *"The Holy Eucharist is the center of our worship (X2)...It is a command that we receive from the Lord."* (X2)
   b. Continue with other songs as the Spirit of the Lord leads.

2. Pray and ask God for the forgiveness of your sins.
   a. Examination of Conscience *(if guilty of any of the following, ask God for mercy and forgiveness)*:
      i. Have I profaned the Body and Blood of the Lord **(1 Corinthians 11:26-27)**?
      ii. Have I received (or been receiving the Eucharist) without honoring Him?

      iii. Do I doubt that the Eucharist is the True Body and Blood of Christ?

      iv. Do I receive the Holy Communion while indulging in a sinful lifestyle?

      v. Do you doubt that partaking of the Eucharist leads to Eternal Life **(John 6:54-56)**?

      vi. Do I receive the Eucharist with gratitude, fully aware of Christ's loving Presence?

      vii. Do I make a visit to the Lord in the Eucharist where He is hidden for love of me?

   b. Pray **Psalm 51** to ask God for the forgiveness of your sins.

3. Put on the full armor of God by praying *"The Warrior's Prayer"* (see page 18).

4. Pray *"The Act of Spiritual Communion"* prayer (see page 19).

5. I cover myself and my household, and the environment of this prayer with the Most Precious Blood of Jesus Christ—in the name of Jesus Christ (7 times).

6. Lord Jesus Christ, I accept You as my way, my truth, and my life. Be my model, my point of reference, and my strength. Without You, I can do nothing; with You, I can do all things—I pray in the name of Jesus Christ.

7. Lord Jesus Christ, I have faith that the broken bread has become for me Your Body broken to make me whole again—I pray in the name of Jesus Christ.

8. Pray and ask the Lord Jesus Christ to give you a Eucharistic Blood transfusion, with His own Precious Blood, in the name of Jesus Christ (pray strongly).

9. Pray for Eucharistic healing (pray "in the name of Jesus Christ"):
   a. Let the Eucharist become a ----- (*pick from the following list*)

destroying all unclean spirits behind every storm I am going through, in the name of Jesus Christ.

- Consuming Fire
- Burning Fire
- Liquid Fire
- Scorching Fire
- Flaming Fire
- Cleansing Fire

b. Let the Eucharist repair and restore every damage that was done to any part of my body, destiny, and talent;

c. Let the Eucharist uproot every weed planted by the enemy in my life;

d. Let the Eucharist release bombshells to the kingdom of darkness that has been troubling my life for ages;

e. Let the Eucharist make my heart like unto the Heart of Jesus;

f. Let the Eucharist make my heart to delight in God and treasure Him alone.

10. I command every foul spirit that has sneaked into my life to leave immediately as I receive the Eucharist, in the name of Jesus Christ.

11. Begin to decree the following in the name of Jesus Christ: Today every ..... (*pick from the following list*) as I encounter Jesus Christ in the Eucharist.
- Dry bone in my life is coming back to life
- Limitation or wall is pulled down
- Dead organ in my body is healed
- Malfunctioning organ in my body is healed
- Embargo in my life is lifted
- Unresolved health is resolved
- Chain in my life is broken
- Stronghold over my life is destroyed

12. As I receive the Eucharist, I am ..... (*pick from the following list*), in the name of Jesus Christ.

- One with Jesus Christ **(John 6:53-56)**
- Receiving the mind of Christ **(Philippians 2:5)**
- Receiving the Life of Jesus Christ **(John 6:53)**
- Receiving His propitiating power **(Romans 3:25)**
- Receiving His purchasing power **(I Peter 1:18-19)**
- Receiving His pacifying power **(Colossians 1 :20)**
- Receiving His cleansing power **(I John 1:7)**
- Receiving His protecting power **(Exodus 12:13)**
- An overcomer **(Revelations 12: 11)**
- Redeemed **(Ephesians 1:7)**
- Justified **(Hebrews 13: 12)**
- Healed indeed **(Isaiah 53:5)**
- Free indeed **(John 8:36)**
- God's sanctuary **(1 Corinthians 3:16)**
- Delivered from darkness
- Made whole

13. I decree that as I receive the Eucharist, I am receiving ..... (*pick from the following list*) into my life—in the name of Jesus Christ.

- Deliverance Medicine
- Divine Vaccination & Immunity
- Divine Surgery
- Immunity booster
- Destroyer of yokes
- Destroyer of a prayerless life
- Divine antibiotics and vitamins
- Blood Cleanser
- Demon Destroyer
- Terminator of terminal illness
- Frustration killer
- Arrester of sickness

14. **Meditation:** When we eat food, it becomes part of us. When we eat Christ in the Eucharist, we become part of Him.

15. I thank You, Lord Jesus Christ, for the successful spiritual warfare granted in this chapter.
    a. I thank You, Lord Jesus Christ, that I have received redemption through Your Most Precious Blood;
    b. I thank You for the deliverance and healing through the Eucharist;
    c. I thank You for providing a long, healthy, and productive life in Your Precious Blood.

16. I cover this prayer with the Most Precious Blood of Jesus Christ (7 times).

Chapter 3

The Holy Eucharist (2)

Very truly I tell you, unless you eat the flesh of the Son of Man and drink His Blood, you have no life in you... Whoever eats My flesh and drinks My Blood remains in me, and I in them."

(John 6:53–56, NIV)

[Other suggested Bible passages to read:
Revelation 1:5, Romans 3:24-25, 1 Peter 1:18-19, John 6:55-59, 1 Corinthians 11:24-30, Isaiah 53:5, Exodus 12:13, Hebrews 13:20-21, Hebrews 12:24, Zechariah 9:11, Ephesians 1:7].

DAY 6 - Part 1: Reflection

In Chapter 2, we saw that the Eucharist is Christ's Real Presence and a powerful weapon against demonic forces. In this chapter, we shall be going deeper in the Power of the Eucharist as a weapon of warfare. We shall be focusing on Eucharistic miracles, healings, deliverances, and testimonies of those who encountered Christ in the Eucharist. One thing stands out as we go through this chapter: The devil cannot stand the Eucharistic Lord! I pray that this chapter will be the last straw to break the stance of any skeptic on the subject of the Eucharist as the scourge of demons.

It was in the year 2015. In one of my retreats at Houston Texas, I encountered a very beautiful lady possessed with marine spirits.

I probed the spirit's identity and I discovered that it was a Queen of the Coast, the commander of the marine kingdom. This spirit charged against me with an unimaginable furiousness, seriously threatening to destroy me if I do not stir clear off her daughter (she calls the lady her daughter). She warned me that she is not in the class of spirits that I have been messing up. I sized her in the spirit and discerned that she was a horrendous spiritual force. With eyes of aggressiveness, she was commanding an air of power. Her threats were beyond words. I haven't seen that kind of threat before! At a point in the deliverance, she began to act and dance coquettishly—a simple way to tell me that I am joking.

I prayed with aggressiveness. She was falling, violently kicking and rolling on the floor, but amidst all these, the spirit remained unmoved and still issuing threats. I prayed but it was like pouring water on a rock. Then, I turned to the Eucharist.

The Eucharist was enthroned at the Altar all this while. I then commanded the lady to gaze intently at the Eucharist Lord, and to my amazement, I saw what blew my mind. Something I could not have imagined! With her body shaking and her eyes seemingly widening as if popping out (while looking intently at the Eucharistic Lord in a way that clearly suggests that she was seeing a Being), she stood straight and gave the Eucharistic Jesus a well-executed military salute!

She held the salute with a deep reverence for a while—as if waiting for a commanding officer to give her the *"At ease"* order. Then to crown it all, while gazing at the Eucharist, she went on her knees and bowed down before the Eucharist with her forehead touching the floor. You don't salute the air, and you don't bow down to *"nothing"*, or do you? Surely, no! You salute someone and bow to a being, for sure. Obviously, she was saluting the Man in the Eucharist. This reminds us of what Apostle Paul told the Philippian Church:

"Therefore God also has highly exalted Him and given Him the name which is above every name, that at the name of Jesus every knee should bow, of those in heaven, and of those on earth, and of those under the earth, and that every tongue should confess that Jesus Christ is Lord, to the glory of God the Father."

(Philippians 2:9-11, NKJV)

If this salute was taking place in a military barrack, you would definitely come to the conclusion that the saluting officer was a person of lower rank (who of course should initiate the salute). In this case, it is also true: the Queen of the coast, the commanding officer of the marine world, is saluting Jesus, the King of Kings—and therefore, Queen of the coast, being an inferior officer and a fallen angel, she had to initiate the salute!

The ordinary eye may see this lady saluting a morsel of *"bread"*, but the Queen of the coast knows that she was not saluting *"something"* but *"Someone"*! She was saluting Jesus Christ, the Commander of the Supreme Headquarters of Heavenly Council, and the General of the Heavenly Armies. This lady was delivered from the power of the Queen of the coast as the Commander of the Heavenly Armies took over.

You see, demons know that Jesus is Lord in the Eucharist. They have no doubt at all! We argue about this but demons don't argue about it at all. While humans may have an intellectual understanding of the Eucharist, demonic spirits have a metaphysical understanding of the Eucharist. They absolutely know the true nature of the Eucharist. Oh yes, demons have true knowledge of Who is in the Eucharist. They know it is not bread or wine, but the Lord Jesus Christ Himself. Demons believe and tremble before the Lord Jesus **(James 2:19)**. In **Mark 3:11**, demons fell down before Jesus saying, ***"You are the Son of God!"*** Jesus rebuked them, notwithstanding bowing down to Him.

The marine spirit in this lady was more aware of the true presence of Jesus in the Eucharist and more astonished by it than the people in the Church that day seeing what was going on. Almost everyone in the pews was stone-dead with fear that day. A man confided in me how he left the front pew and went to stand by the door, should the spirit become apocalyptic. He thought he was safer at the door than right inside the Church. What a contradiction of faith that someone who came to encounter the Savior of his soul would run away from His Presence for fear. Believing intellectually in the true presence is not enough: it is far more wonderful when we believe in the depth of our soul. It is so easy for us to act with the sense of indifference in the presence of the Eucharist, forgetful of the miraculous and awesome Presence available to us!

On this note, I wish to share with you an article I recently came across in which a Priest described an experience he had during Mass when he lifted the Chalice (The Blood of Jesus Christ). The article narrates[2]:

> *"Then, I heard another sound, this time an undeniable moan and then a shriek as someone cried out, 'Leave me alone, Jesus! Why do you torture me?' Suddenly there was a scuffling noise and someone ran out [of the Church] with the groaning sound of having been injured. The back doors swung open and then closed. Then silence...I knew in an instant that some poor demon-tormented soul had encountered Christ in the Eucharist and could not endure His real presence displayed for all to see."*

I was attending Mass when I witnessed the power of the Holy Eucharist in a way similar to the Priest's experience in the article described above. I am not sure of the year this happened, but definitely, an event that happened between 2005 and 2007. On my way to work, I entered my Parish to attend morning Mass as it was my custom[3]. After consecration, we were on a single file

2. https://onepeterfive.com/what-demons-know-about-the-eucharist-that-many-catholics-dont/
3. St. Jude Catholic Church, Rumuokoro, Port Harcourt, Nigeria

receiving Holy Communion from the Priest. There were about two or three persons ahead of me waiting for their turn to receive Holy Communion when, all of a sudden, a commotion arose at the point when a middle-aged man proceeded to receive Holy Communion.

As the Priest displayed the Eucharist and said "The Body of Christ" to this man who was standing before him about to receive Communion, his response was not "Amen" as was expected of him, but a sudden outburst of a scream at the top of his voice followed by some quick staggers as if struggling with an invisible person. Almost immediately, a great force threw him to the floor. He laid on the floor for some time and got up with a marked trepidation on his face. All eyes were on him as this was no small thing! The Priest was taken aback, wondering what that could mean. Afterward, calmness returned, and we continued receiving Holy Communion.

At the end of the Mass, the Priest interviewed the man and he confessed to our hearing a shocking story that motivated me to share this event in this book so as to throw more light on the tremendous power of the Eucharist. According to this man, he said he came to Port Harcourt to attend a ritual meeting of the secret cult group that he joined because he wanted to become rich as his suffering was becoming too much for him to bear. This was his first time coming to Port Harcourt. During the midnight ritual, there was a misunderstanding between him and the occult group as he was asked to sacrifice his mother by stabbing her image that appeared in a basin of water (this was at a major road intersection along Choba-Warri road). *"I love my mother so much and I cannot sacrifice her for money,"* he said. He continued:

> *"I was threatened that if I do not sacrifice my mother, I was going to be killed. Fearing for my life, I ran away and was able to escape from them. Not being to Port Harcourt before, I was walking aimlessly along the road all night when in the early morning I saw a gate flung open and*

discovered that a lot of people were entering this place. I joined them and found out that it was a Church. I entered the Church and sat down on the pew. They were praying (he was referring to the Morning Mass) and when people stood up to take 'something' from the priest, I also got up and joined them thinking that it was for everyone. When it was my turn to receive the thing that people were receiving, a powerful force came out of it and threw me on the ground."

This occult man had an encounter with the Power of Jesus in the Eucharist. Jesus in the Eucharist is the same *"Man of war"* who fought the ancient wars and came back with victory **(Exodus 15:3, NKJV)**. In the Eucharist, He is still a *"Man of war"* fighting the occult kingdoms and their forces. The kingdom of darkness cannot stand the Eucharistic Jesus, not even for a moment.

In the Old Testament, the Holy of Holies is the inner sanctuary of the Tabernacle where God's Presence appeared. After Consecration, the bread (now Eucharist) becomes *Sanctissimum* (Latin)—which means the "Most Holy" or "Holy of Holies"—and only God can take this title. In the Old Testament, people who approached God's Holy of Holies unauthorized— like the occult man whose story I just narrated— dropped dead **(2 Samuel 6:7)**. The devil sees not bread in the *Sanctissimum* but the very One who conquered him on the Cross at Calvary.

God who would not allow Moses to see His Face—for *"no one may see me and live"* **(Exodus 33:20)**— has now allowed us to, not only see Him in the Eucharist, but to even approach, touch, and receive Him in the Eucharist in order to have life. God struck a man dead who tried to protect the Ark of God from falling **(2 Samuel 6:3-8; 1 Chronicles 13:6-12)**. In this era of grace, we receive Him in the Eucharist sharing in His Divine Life as to become one in body and spirit with Him! Never in the history of mankind was it possible to touch God but in ours. We live in an era of grace brought to us by Jesus Christ. Praise God! Alleluia!!

THE HOLY EUCHARIST (2)

I cannot conclude this chapter without mentioning what the world-renowned Televangelist Benny Hinn said regarding Eucharistic healing (his ministry focuses on healing). In addressing his Pentecostal audience, he said[4]:

> "They just released a study that more people are healed in a Catholic Church than in Pentecostal churches. The studies have proven it. [This is] because Catholic people revere the Eucharist. More people get healed in a Catholic Church during communion than Pentecostals... because to us it's symbolic. Well, Jesus didn't say, 'This is symbolic of Body,' He said, 'This is My Body'; [He didn't say,] 'This is symbolic of My Blood,' He said, 'This is My Blood...And I believe, I always have believed... There's healing in communion... And there's healing in the Catholic Churches because these people are devoted and show up every Sunday... and many of them are healed."

Benny Hinn clearly relates to the power of the Eucharist to heal because in the Eucharist is the Real Presence of Jesus Christ! You will not have a problem believing what Jesus says about the Eucharist if you sincerely seek understanding from Him. You will discover the Lord in the Eucharist if you seek revelation knowledge in this matter. Many Christians, like the two disciples on their way to Emmaus, are sincerely serving the Lord but really not seeing Him in their walk of faith. It was by revelation during the Eucharistic meal that the men on their way to Emmaus recognized that He was the Lord Jesus Christ (Luke 24:29-31). Listening to Christ on the way prepared these two disciples to recognize Him in the breaking of the bread. After recognizing Him in the "breaking of the bread" (the Eucharist), their entire dispositions changed: They had stopped for the evening to catch some rest (Luke 24:28-29), but after experiencing the Lord

---

4. https://www.youtube.com/watch?v=VvYeXh3JHco

in the Eucharist, *"they rose up that very hour and returned to Jerusalem"* to share their experience with others **(Luke 24:33-35)**.

Likewise, listening to Jesus will reveal His Real Presence in the Eucharist to us—and our entire dispositions will also change! Even a doubting Thomas would not doubt that Jesus is Lord in the Eucharist when the grace of revelational knowledge is granted him. It was a revelation that took away Thomas' doubt that the crucified Lord had become the risen Lord **(John 20: 24- 29)**. Jesus is still telling skeptics, *"stop doubting and believe"* (John 20:27). Had the Bible not revealed the truth about the Eucharist, my personal revelations on this subject are sufficient enough for me to know that the Eucharist is Christ's Real Presence. What a gift from God! In fact, the Eucharist is not only a gift from God but the Gift Who is God. It is the greatest of all gifts!

The devil has deceived most Christians into believing that the Eucharist is symbolic of God's Presence, and not His Real Presence. You know, think about it—when Jesus changed water into wine as narrated in **John 2:1-11,** was it symbolic or was the wine real? We know the answer, don't we? He changed the water to a real wine. So why would the change of wine to Blood become a symbol? Really, this thing is not complicated when we allow God to enlighten us. My dear friend, let's then ask The Holy Spirit to lead us through understanding Biblical mysteries like the Holy Eucharist.

This reminds me of an aged mother who was desperate to see her two grown-up girls get married. For years, she had prayed and wept but the situation prevailed. Upon sharing her ordeal with her friend, she was advised to go and tell Jesus about it in the Blessed Sacrament (i.e. The Eucharist exposed in a monstrance). She took what her friend told her literally, and went to the Blessed Sacrament Chapel to meet Jesus as she was told. The first day she went to the Chapel, she saw so many people kneeling and praying before the Blessed Sacrament. She knelt and prayed, *"Jesus, please, give my children their husbands."* She did this for three days. On the third day, after her prayers, she left the Chapel as usual. Surprisingly, this time, she fell on the ground at the door entrance of the Chapel. People rushed to her immediately, thinking she needed help. Not long, after regaining her conscious self, she told them what happened. Hear her story:

> *"My friend told me to come and meet Jesus in the Blessed Sacrament and tell Him my problems. I have not been to the Blessed Sacrament Chapel before. I have not heard about it before either. The first day I came, I saw a Man sitting on a Throne wearing White and smiling at me. I knew He was Jesus Christ that everyone in the Chapel was praying to. I prayed to Him, asking Him to help my children get married. He smiled and told me that He has answered me. As I was leaving, He opted to see me off. We both walked towards the entrance door of the Chapel. At the door, He stood and bade me a bye. The same thing happened on the second and on the third day, except that today (third day), when I stepped out of the Chapel and turned for us to bid each other a bye, as usual, I saw Him magnified too big that the whole Chapel could not contain Him. I was shocked as I couldn't stand what I saw. It appeared I had no strength left and fell into a slumber."*

Her story startled everyone. She saw Jesus where others saw "Bread". This woman was very surprised to learn later that the other people with her in the Chapel did not see Who she saw. This woman, a non-Catholic, being ignorant of the Blessed Sacrament, however, like a little child expecting some candies from Father Christmas on a Christmas Eve, without doubt, believed her friend when she told her that Jesus is in the Blessed Sacrament. Perhaps, we need to go to kids and learn how to believe what God says, instead of subjecting it to intellectual scrutiny.

Shortly after this woman's experience, her two girls got married at the same time. She gave her testimony in Church and it motivated people to take the Eucharist more seriously. My dear, Jesus is in the Blessed Sacrament to answer your prayers. If we would focus on the Eucharist as the actual Body and the actual Blood of Jesus Christ, the blessings of the new covenant would manifest in our lives.

Keeping the Body of Christ divided in the very center of Christians' power is nothing short of a successful attack against the Church. It is also a successful attack against the Body of Christ when Christians believe everything else in the Bible as God said it but not the Eucharist. It pains the heart of Jesus to see us divided among ourselves over the gift of Himself that is meant to unite us. It pains Him that the Eucharist He gave to us to fight the kingdom of darkness is kept in the scabbard. It should not be doubted that when the enemy succeeds in keeping the Body of Christ divided over what Jesus said, the same enemy uses what Jesus didn't say to fight God's people.

It pains Him most for every rejection, mockery, or blasphemy of the Eucharist in our contemporary time. For instance, abortion is a mockery of the Eucharist. The very Holy Words that Jesus used in giving us the Eucharist *"This is My Body"* **(Luke 22:19)** is the same words abortionists use to justify their heinous evil: *"This is my body... so why shouldn't I be able to do what I want with it."* Abortion is also a negation of the Eucharist: The Eucharist gives life; abortion takes life.

I do not have the luxury of time and space to write on the many Eucharistic miracles, healings, and deliverances that abound in the Church—and all of them are eloquent testimonies of the overwhelming power of the Eucharist. Many miracles are being harvested daily from encounters with the Eucharistic Lord through daily Eucharistic activities. To discover the Eucharistic Lord is to discover a priceless treasure! The Psalmist describes how *"The poor shall eat and be satisfied"* **(Psalm 22:26)**. On earth, we are all poor, separated from God.

There is only one thing that can truly fill us, body and spirit— the Eucharist! Every day, Jesus sits with us at the Eucharistic table dispensing healing, deliverance, and other divine benefits to His children. The Lord, surely, has prepared a Eucharistic table before us for a Meal. Let us come to the table upon His invitation to eat His Sacred Body and drink His Sacred Blood for the refreshment and strengthening of our souls. When we do this, we receive the power to conquer our enemies. Let us make the Eucharist our companion! Let us be wise!

[It is recommended that you make the following prayers before the Eucharistic Lord if you have the grace and the opportunity to do so. You might also decide to conclude the prayer and then receive the Holy Eucharist (following the proper procedure of the Church to receive Holy Communion)].

LET US PRAY!
1. Reflect on how this reflection on *"The Holy Eucharist"* ministers to you.
   a. Reflect on **Isaiah 25:6** which says, *"On this mountain, the LORD of hosts will provide for all peoples a feast of rich food and choice wines, juicy, rich food and pure, choice wines"*;
   b. Reflect on **Isaiah 55:1-3** which says, *"All you who are thirsty, come to the water! You who have no money, come, receive grain and eat; Come, without paying and without cost, drink wine and milk! Why spend your money for what is not bread; your wages for what fails to satisfy? Heed me, and you shall eat well, you shall delight in rich fare. Come to me heedfully, listen, that you may have life. I will renew with you the everlasting covenant, the benefits assured to David."*
   c. Reflect on **Ezekiel 3:1-4** which says, *"He said to me: Son of man, eat what is before you; eat this scroll, then go, speak to*

the house of Israel. So I opened my mouth and he gave me the scroll to eat. Son of man, he then said to me, feed your belly and fill your stomach with this scroll I am giving you. I ate it, and it was as sweet as honey in my mouth. He said: Son of man, go now to the house of Israel, and speak my words to them."

2. Pray and ask God for the forgiveness of your sins using **Psalm 51.**

3. Put on the full armor of God by praying *"The Warrior's Prayer"* (see page 18).

4. Pray *"The Act of Spiritual Communion"* prayer (see page 19).

5. Pray **Psalm 23** and reflect on verse 5 where the Lord promises to prepare a table for you in the presence of the enemies.

6. Lord Jesus, help me value more the gift of Yourself in the Eucharist.

7. *"If only I possessed the grace, good Jesus, to be utterly one with You! Amidst all the variety of worldly things around me, Lord, the only thing I crave is unity with You. You are all my soul needs. Unite, dear friend of my heart, this unique little soul of mine to Your perfect goodness [in the Blessed Eucharist]. You are all mine; when shall I be Yours? Lord Jesus, my beloved, be the magnet of my heart; clasp, press, and unite me forever to Your Sacred Heart. You have made me for Yourself; make me one with You. Absorb this tiny drop of life into the ocean of goodness whence it came."* (Prayer of Francis de Sales, 1567-1622).

8. Pray with the Roman Centurion: ***"Lord, I am not worthy to have You come under my roof, but only speak the Word, and my servant will be healed"*** **(Matthew 8:8).** The Centurion expressed his deep faith in the Lord's healing Power. Jesus was quite moved

by the Centurion's faith, and healed his servant at once! (Please note that Jesus might not answer us quite so instantaneously, but we ought to be rest-assured that He can and will respond in His own time and manner to anyone who comes to Him in love and humility for His Divine assistance. After all, He tells us, *"Ask, and it will be given you; search, and you will find; knock, and the door will be opened for you"* (**Matthew 7:7**). Therefore, in the name of Jesus Christ:

   a.   Pray and ask Him for your healing;

   b.   Pray for the healing of those who are sick.

9.   Thank You Lord Jesus Christ for answering my prayers. I cover this prayer with the Most Precious Blood of Jesus Christ (7 times).

DAY 7 - Part 2: Warfare Prayers

Note:

- The Lord Jesus gives us a great opportunity to be with Him on a daily basis through the Eucharist. Think of it: Can any wall shut us out from the good Lord? Is there anything in this world that could ever be like having a private "audience" with Jesus Christ upon receiving Him in Holy Communion or in spiritual communion in front of the Blessed Sacrament? There are great spiritual virtues and benefits you will receive every time you spent with our Lord in the Eucharist. Remember, however, that you can "turn toward the Eucharist" and receive Jesus in your heart from anywhere you might happen to be, at any time, day or night! It is an act very pleasing to God. Practice this!

- **Resolution:** Decide today to have a passion for the Eucharist. Draw strength from Him.

- **Assignment:** Anytime you receive the Eucharist, you should say, *"The life of God is manifesting in my body"* or *"By His stripes, I am healed"* or *"The Lord's Body is broken for my healing"* or *"I am becoming one in body and spirit with Jesus Christ."* Sing songs as led by the Holy Spirit (You may start with singing some Eucharistic songs or songs that exalt the Most Precious Blood of Jesus Christ).

1. O fountain of all mercy, visit me with Your salvation. Pray **Psalm 51** for the forgiveness of your sins:
   a. Repent of focusing on the *"wretched food"* of this world, which leads to grumbling **(Numbers 21:5)**;
   b. From this moment on, I choose to stay fully surrendered to my Lord Jesus Christ all the days of my life. I confess that the Holy Eucharist is the center of my life, in the name of Jesus Christ.

2. Put on the full armor of God by praying *"The Warrior's Prayer"* (see page 18).

3. Pray *"The Act of Spiritual Communion"* prayer (see page 19).

4. *"Here, O good and gentle Jesus, I kneel before you, and with all the fervor of my soul I pray that you engrave within my heart lively sentiments of faith, hope, and love, true repentance for my sins, and a firm purpose of amendment. While I see and I ponder your five wounds with great affection and sorrow in my soul, I have before my eyes those words of yours that David prophesied about you:* **'They have pierced my hands and feet; I can count all my bones'** *(Psalm 22:17)"*— **Roman Missal.**

5. Lord Jesus Christ, come spiritually into my heart. Purify it. Sanctify it. Render it like unto Your own, in the name of Jesus Christ. Amen!

6. **"I would feed you with the finest of the wheat, and with honey**

from the rock, I would satisfy you" (Psalm 81:16). Lord Jesus, you satisfy the deepest longing of our hearts and you feed us with the finest of wheat. Therefore, Lord (pray "in the name of Jesus Christ"):

a. Satisfy the deepest longing and hunger in my heart;

b. May I always hunger for the imperishable bread, that I may be satisfied in You alone as the True Bread of Heaven;

c. Nourish and strengthen me that I may serve You with great joy, generosity, and zeal all the days of my life.

7. Lord Jesus Christ, You are the living Bread which sustains me in this life. May I always hunger for the bread which comes from heaven and find in it the nourishment and strength that I need to love and serve You wholeheartedly—in the name of Jesus Christ.

8. Lord Jesus Christ, You are the Bread of life and the source of Eternal life **(John 6:54-56)**. May I receive You as to become like You, in the name of Jesus Christ.

9. Lord Jesus Christ, prepare my heart for a true communion with You, in the name of Jesus Christ.

10. Lord Jesus Christ, give us this day our daily bread. Give us more of You, the Bread of Life—in the name of Jesus Christ.

11. The Eucharist reminds us that the power of the enemy has been defeated. Therefore, as I come before Jesus in the Eucharist------- *(pick from the following list)* has been defeated, in the name of Jesus Christ.

- Sickness
- Addiction
- Failure
- Fear
- Divorce
- Discouragement
- Hopelessness
- Satan (your enemy)
- Continue as the Spirit leads

12. Lord **Jesus Christ,** You alone can satisfy the deepest longing and hunger in my heart. Pray the following in the name of Jesus Christ:
    a. May I always hunger for the imperishable bread, that I may be satisfied in You alone as the True Bread of Heaven;
    b. Nourish and strengthen me that I may serve you with great joy, generosity, and zeal all the days of my life.

13. I thank You, Lord Jesus Chris, for the victory granted me in this spiritual warfare.
    a. Thank You for accompanying us with love as we journey through life, always present among us.
    b. Thank You for Your love that gathers us together in the Eucharist.

14. I cover this prayer with the Most Precious Blood of Jesus Christ (7 times).

Chapter 4

The Power of Sacrifice

"When the king heard what the man of God cried out against the altar at Bethel, Jeroboam stretched out his hand from the altar, saying, "Seize him!" But the hand that he stretched out against him withered so that he could not draw it back to himself. The altar also was torn down, and the ashes poured out from the altar, according to the sign that the man of God had given by the word of the Lord"

(1 Kings 13:4-5)

[Other suggested Bible passages to read: Hebrews 13:1-16, Romans 12:1, 1 Kings 18:16-40, Psalm 51:16-19, 2 Samuel 24:25, John 15:13, Ephesians 5:2, Hebrews 9:28, Luke 9:24, Proverbs 21:3, Matthew 9:13, Jonah 2:9].

DAY 8 - Part 1: Reflection

I want to share something deep with you in this chapter. It is about sacrifice. And I would like to start by asking you to think about what brought salvation to those in the ship with Jonah. I want to introduce you to how powerful sacrifice is by probing into that which is often ignored when Preachers talk about Jonah in the ship. I want to make a case here that it was a "sacrifice" that saved the lives of the people in the ship.

As we are aware, a great wind came upon the sea, and the ship carrying Jonah with other voyagers threatened to break up **(Jonah 1:4)**. The people were very afraid and began to make a sacrifice of prayer as *"each cried to his god"* (Jonah 1:5a). Yet the storm prevailed. Then they "sacrificed" their belongings by throwing *"the cargo that was in the ship into the sea, to lighten it for them"* **(Jonah 1:5b)**, and yet the great wind was threatening to sink their ship. In the state of this frenzy, the captain of the ship discovered Jonah fast asleep and upon waking him up, charged him saying, *"Get up, call on your god!"* (Jonah 1:6).

Upon discovering that the storm was because of Jonah running away from the Lord, they asked him: *"What shall we do to you, that the sea may quiet down for us?"* **(Jonah 1:11a)**. For this Jonah said to them, *"Pick me up and throw me into the sea; then the sea will quiet down for you"* **(Jonah 1:12)**. Nevertheless the men wanted to save Jonah, and so they *"rowed hard to bring the ship back to land"* **(Jonah 1:13a)**—again, they "sacrificed" their time and strength *"but they could not, for the sea grew more and more stormy against them"* **(Jonah 1:13b)**.

Then after praying to God not to hold them *"guilty of innocent blood...they picked Jonah up and threw him into the sea"* **(Jonah 1:14)** —again, they made a "sacrifice". This time, *"the sea ceased from its raging"* **(Jonah 1:15)**. Then the people *"offered a sacrifice to the Lord and made vows"* **(Jonah 1:16)** —again, they made a sacrifice, the sacrifice of thanksgiving!

Let's look more closely into this story. In order for the ship to be saved, the sailors understood that Jonah had to be thrown into the sea. This is a type of sacrifice! This is a prophetic picture of salvation. Those in the ship tried to save themselves by making the sacrifices of prayer to their *god* **(Jonah 1:5)**, but all to no avail because they were making the wrong sacrifice. Professional swimmers were there in the ship, but they could neither save themselves nor reach the shore of salvation on their own merit! This is a candid pointer that mankind cannot save itself.

All the efforts made by the people to save themselves were in vain until the right *"sacrifice"* was made. Jonah was *"sacrificed"* before the voyage could reach the shore of salvation. This is alluding to the fact that Someone has to be *"sacrificed"* before the ship of humanity shall safely make it to the shores of salvation. Someone must die that we may live— because, by our own efforts, we are incapable of saving ourselves. Only God can save man; man cannot save himself. Man is helpless without God!

The above story of how salvation came to the sea travelers by *"sacrificing"* Jonah presents a clear and undeniable fact that sacrifice is a powerful thing. An Altar is a place where you call on your God (or gods for unbelievers). Altars are like doors. They are doors to the spiritual world. With it, you can access the supernatural world.

Altars are powered by sacrifice done on them. The right sacrifice brings spiritual victory, much like the sacrifice of Jonah opened the door of answered prayers for the sea travelers. Jesus' parting words, *"It is finished!"* **(John 19:30)** expresses a rightly-pleasing and fully completed sacrifice that brings forth victory for mankind. Jesus bowed His head and gave up His spirit knowing that His Father had accepted His sacrifice and that the battle was won.

It was Elijah's sacrifice at the altar that brought victory to him over the evil forces of Baal **(1 Kings 18: 30-40)**. The sacrifice of prayer took place on the altar before that monumental victory, not the other way round. My dear, listen: The devil dreads the Cross, not because it was a cross—for crosses had always been— but because of the sacrifice on it at Calvary. This is important to understand!

Your altar is as powerful as your sacrifice of prayer. Does this help us understand why *"The Lord spoke to Moses, saying: 'Command Aaron and his sons, saying...The fire on the altar shall be kept burning; it shall not go out'"* **(Leviticus 6:8-9, 12)**. Just as *"Without wood, a fire goes out"* **(Proverbs 26:20, NIV)**, so without the sacrifice of prayer, an Altar becomes powerless (you may refer to it as an altar without fire).

There are many invisible arrows that are flying in the spiritual realm, but sacrifice decides where they go to. Jeroboam stretched out his hand from his altar against a Prophet of God, but the sacrifice at the altar of the man of God directed the evil arrow sent to seize the man of God back to the sender (King Jeroboam), and caused his hand (Jeroboam's) to wither *"so that he could not draw it back to himself"* (1 Kings 13:4). *"The [evil] altar also was torn down, and the ashes poured out from the altar, according to the sign that the man of God had given by the word of the Lord"* (1 Kings 13:5). The evil altar was altered by someone's sacrifice of prayer! Let your Altar alter the altar of darkness.

Again, I wish to repeat myself: Sacrifice is powerful!

Through sacrifice, the altar opens the spiritual doors and begins to speak—much like an open mouth talks. Many Christians are not aware that altars speak. Altars do have a voice. Evil altars speak evil against the saints of God (see the case of 1 Kings 13:4-5), while the Altar of the Living God speaks the Blood of Jesus Christ. This is a sufficient incentive to attach your life to the Altar of God.

No demon can fight you in your sanctuary. In the Old Testament Jewish Altar of worship, there is a protrusion at each corner of the Altar called the horn of the Altar (Exodus 27:2). During worship session, the horns of the Altar were dabbed with blood to purify them and make atonement for sins (Leviticus 8:15). When this sacrifice is done, the Altar (the horns of the altar) begins to "speak" of the power of God's salvation—hence, the Psalmist rightly called it *"the horn of my salvation, my stronghold"* (Psalm 18:2). That part of the altar also becomes a place of refuge and sanctuary for a fugitive (1 Kings 1:50).

Anyone running to the Altar and holding the horns of the Altar cannot be harmed by the enemy. The horn of our salvation is stronger than the enemy, no matter how strong the enemy might be. Jesus Christ is the horn of our salvation **(Luke 1:68–69)**. In fact, the very name Jesus means *"The Lord Is Salvation!"* Matthew 1:21 rightly says, *"For He [Jesus] will save His people from their sins."* The salvation Jesus offers is strong, triumphant, and powerful—but that salvation came to us by way of sacrifice. Just like the horns on the Altar offered refuge and atonement, Jesus, through His sacrificial death on the Cross, offers clemency and cleansing.

You see how powerful an Altar could be, yet what empowers the altar is the sacrifice done on it. The kingdom of darkness understands very well the spiritual reality that sacrifices make altars to speak—and so they make diabolical sacrifices on their evil altars! In fact, altars cannot speak without a sacrifice. Are you still surprised that altars can speak?

Although sacrifice could be done with many elements (e.g., Cain sacrificed crops on his own altar), blood sacrifice is more powerful, especially human blood, and most especially the primal sacrifice of *"innocent blood"* (actually, the sacrifice of innocent children). Actually, using children for sacrifice is not new. It had been a practice from the ancient times, for *"They would even burn their sons and their daughters in the fire to their gods* **(Deuteronomy 12:32)**. God warned the Israelites in **Leviticus 18:21**, *"You shall not give any of your offspring to sacrifice them to Molech."* The kingdom of darkness understands this very well and has over history till date, been sacrificing with human blood. In our time, the sacrifice of innocent blood has taken a new shape through abortion.

However, the grand climax of sacrifice on an altar is human blood without stain of sin. Children have innocent blood but have blood that is stained with original sin on the grounds that *"all have sinned"* **(Romans 3:23)**. Where would God get such stainless blood for a sacrifice that would bring redemption for mankind since such blood must be *"without defect or blemish"* (**1 Peter 1:19**)? Definitely, such blood cannot come from the children of Adam for *"all have sinned and fall short of the glory of God"* (**Romans 3:23**). And not the blood of animals because animals' blood is inferior to human blood (Abel's offering, in **Genesis 4:4**, involved the sacrifice of a lamb and with it the shedding of its blood, but it cannot atone for the sins of the entire humanity), and of course grain offering, which is ruled out because its sacrificing potency is inferior to even the blood of animals.

To solve this problem, God Himself decided to become a Man without any iota of sin in Him. His name is Jesus Christ, the Lamb of God. The Blood of Jesus met the Divine requirement for man's salvation: Blood without sin. Being sacrificed on the Cross, Jesus Christ becomes the just dying for the unjust, and the innocent dying for the guilty sinners. This sacrifice inputs upon us the righteousness of God through Christ (**Romans 3:22**). It is as if we wear the garment of righteousness bought with the unblemished Blood of Jesus Christ.

Genesis 4:4 describes the first worship service and God's acceptance of sacrifice in worship—and this was a blood sacrifice! [This alludes to the fact that God is to be worshipped through sacrifice: Be it the sacrifice of praise, worship, or prayer; be it the sacrifice of our lives or bodies, or doing good and sharing with others]. Sacrifice reveals what and who we really love. Abraham's willingness to sacrifice his son, Isaac, not only proved his faith, but also his supreme love for God. Jesus' death on the Cross is the evidence of His love for us.

There's no true love without sacrifice. We cannot actually serve God without making sacrifices. Every Christian life must incorporate a healthy spirit of sacrifice and self-denial. Jesus is still looking for the few who are willing to commit out-of-the-ordinary, intentional acts of selfless sacrifice so that He can turn their sacrifice into His glory. Commit such an act today! Jesus talked about this sacrifice when He told His disciples: *"And everyone who has left houses or brothers or sisters or father or mother or children or fields, for my name's sake, will receive a hundredfold, and will inherit eternal life"* (Matthew 19:29). Actually, no sacrifice we make is too great for the One who sacrificed His all for us—Jesus Christ! Jesus Christ by His sacrifice put away sin, defeated the stronghold of suffering, and ultimately destroyed death—in all Himself.

On the day that Jesus sacrificed His life on the Cross of Calvary, the sun sacrificed its light in honor of Him who gave it its light (Luke 23:44, Mark 15:33), the temple veil rent (Matthew 27:51), the earth shook, and the rocks shattered in honor of The Rock of Ages (Matthew 27:51). Similarly, like the sun sacrificing its light (its gift), we ought to offer sacrifices of our gifts to Jesus's Sacrifice.

Just as Godly worship is made through sacrifice, Satan's system of worship is also based on sacrifice. This is very important for us to understand! Satanic worship is very deep. Unfortunately, I do not have room here to navigate into this vampire-world of heinous sacrifices. With rising interests in the occult, witchcraft, and other satanic faculties, it cannot be overemphasized that our sacrifice of prayer should speak for us in the spiritual battlefield.

LET US PRAY!
1. Reflect on how this reflection on *"The Power of Sacrifice"* ministers to you.

2. Pray and ask God for the forgiveness of your sins using **Psalm 51.**

3. Put on the full armor of God by praying *"The Warrior's Prayer"* (see page 18).

4. Pray *"The Act of Spiritual Communion"* prayer (see page 19).

5. Pray **Psalm 50** (a prayer for an acceptable sacrifice to God).

6. Close your eyes and meditate on the sacrificial death of Jesus Christ on the hills of Calvary, and then begin to pray. Ask God to lead you in this spiritual battlefield that you are getting into now.

    a. I stand at the foot of the Cross, and I submit to the authority of Christ's Majesty as I make this prayer;

    b. Lord Jesus Christ, I humbly prostrate myself at the foot of the Cross;

    c. Lord Jesus Christ, You know the troubles that I am going through all these years. Now, I lay these burdens at the foot of the Cross *(present the situation to the Lord and leave them at the foot of the Cross)*. They are no more mine—in the name of Jesus Christ;

    d. Lord Jesus Christ, I ask that the Altar of Calvary shall begin to speak the Blood of Jesus Christ over my life as I engage in this prayer;

    e. I cover myself with the Blood and Water that are gushing forth from the sacred side of my Lord Jesus Christ *(repeat 3 times);*

    f. I summon to the Altar of Calvary and set on fire all the assets of the devil that are used against me and my loved ones: strongholds, shrines, temples, evil altars, evil forests and rivers, witchcraft covens, charms, demonic priests, and deities;

    g. Standing on the providence of the sacrifice of Jesus Christ on the Cross, I decree that:

        i.   Every pathway that has allowed Satan and his demons into my life is closed;

        ii. Every legal right that the devil holds against my life is annulled;

        iii. The Divine radiation emanating from the Sacred Heart of Jesus Christ is healing me and every other sick person now *(mention their names);*

    iv. The Blood of Jesus Christ that is gushing forth from the pierced side of Jesus Christ is covering my family, my family roots, my friends, my relationships, my house, my properties and all that belongs to me;

    v. The wounds in the pierced hands of Jesus is healing me now:

- Lord Jesus Christ, please heal the pains in my wounded heart;
- I offer You the condition of my heart: Please accept it and make it Your sanctuary.

h. Meditate on the wounds of Christ on His head, hands, feet, back, and side. Pray the following prayers (making each prayer in the name of Jesus Christ):

    i. The Blood from Christ's head when the thorns pierced His Sacred head shields my head from every fiery arrow of the evil one **(Ephesians 6:16)**;

    ii. The Blood from Christ's pierced hands frees me from the chains on my hands **(Jeremiah 40:4)**;

    iii. The Blood from Christ's pierced feet breaks *"the chains that hold us back and throw off the ropes that tie us down"* **(Psalm 2:3, NCV)**;

    iv. The Blood from Christ's lacerated Body heals me and destroys every sting of death;

    v. The Blood from Christ's pierced side is sanctifying me and my household.

i. In the name of Jesus Christ (*as I take a stand at the foot of the Cross*), I summon, by way of command, every demonic element to go immediately under the foot of the Cross of Jesus Christ to be disposed of according to God's Holy Will. [Then begin to pray as follows, ending every prayer with "*in the Name of Jesus Christ, Amen.*"]:

    i. I bind all evil spirits that are hiding in the air, water, earth, under the earth and infernal world. I invoke the Precious Blood of Jesus Christ that is gushing forth from the Body of Jesus Christ in the air, the atmosphere, the water, the land, and its fruits. I command all you evil powers to perish now;

ii. I bind all demonic spies sent against me from all satanic quarters. I command you all to perish;

iii. I break, I shatter, and I cancel every curse, betrayal, enchantment, spell, trap, lie, obstacle, evil arrows, hereditary blockage (known or unknown), manipulations or evil desire that are projected at me by the forces of darkness to cause me misfortune. I command all you evil powers to perish now;

iv. I cancel every attachment to the devil and I disengage myself today from any known or unknown association or relationship with the powers of the evil.

j. O you evil transfers and communication between evil altars in my bloodline for generations now, I command you to seize and never to communicate with each other again;

k. Lord Jesus Christ has disarmed the devil of his deadly power. Therefore, the devil and his demons have no power over my life, in the name of Jesus Christ, Amen.

7. Thank You Lord Jesus Christ for answering my prayers. I cover this prayer with the Most Precious Blood of Jesus Christ (7 times).

DAY 9 - Part 2: Warfare Prayers

Note:
- Love is powerful, and so is sacrifice powerful. Yet, the genuineness and depth of love is tested by our sacrifice. There's no true love without sacrifice.

- Our redemption is made possible by the sacrifice of Jesus Christ on the Cross of Calvary.

- Having an Altar of God in your house is encouraged. The explanations in this chapter explain why it is important to do so.

1. Lord Jesus, I worship You, and I give You praise. I recognize that You are worthy to receive all glory, honor, and praise **(Revelation 4:11).**

    a. I surrender myself completely and unreservedly to the Holy Spirit to lead me into victory through this prayer;

    b. Praise and worship God as the Holy Spirit leads you.

2. *"The sacrifice acceptable to God is a broken spirit; a broken and contrite heart, O God, You will not despise"* **(Psalm 51:17).** Therefore, with a contrite spirit, ask God to have mercy on you as you offer your sins to Him.

    a. Examination of Conscience *(if guilty of any of the following, ask God for mercy and forgiveness):*
        i. Have I or my ancestors made sacrifices that honored the devil?
        ii. Do I make sacrifices for the good of others?
        iii. Do I fail to make a sacrifice of doing good and sharing my God-given gifts generously with others?
        iv. Does my lifestyle dishonor the sacrificial death of Jesus Christ on the Cross?
        v. Do I fail to make sacrifices of praise, worship, and prayer for a deeper relationship with God?

    b. Pray Psalm 51 to ask God for the forgiveness of your sins;

    c. From this moment on, I choose to stay fully surrendered to my Lord Jesus Christ all the days of my life.

3. Put on the full armor of God by praying *"The Warrior's Prayer"* (see page 18).

4. Pray *"The Act of Spiritual Communion"* prayer (see page 19).

5. I cover myself and my household, and the environment of this prayer with the Most Precious Blood of Jesus Christ—in the name of Jesus Christ (7 times).

6. Satanic sacrifices at crossroads are often used to either project or summon demons from the North, South, East, and West against a person. Pray against such satanic projections or summons from the four cardinal points of the earth. Therefore, in the name of Jesus Christ, I decree that:

    a. The Altar of Jesus Christ's sacrifice on the hill of Calvary has made powerless and useless every evil altar that is raised at crossroads to summon me and my loved ones by satanic sacrifices;

    b. Every dominion of the devil is on fire right now:
        i. Every celestial space be grounded, in the name of Jesus Christ;
        ii. Every sacred rivers dry up, in the name of Jesus Christ;
        iii. Every sacred mountains be leveled down, in the name of Jesus Christ;
        iv. Every evil forest burn to ashes, in the name of Jesus Christ.

    c. Every satanic projection against my spirit is destroyed.

7. I refuse to... (*pick from the following*) when summoned, in the name of Jesus Christ.

    - Appear to the altar of evil judgment
    - Appear in demonic mirrors
    - Appear in demonic altars
    - Engage with a demonic spouse
    - Drink the water of bitterness
    - Appear to the altar of condemnation
    - Be nailed down to stagnation
    - Appear in satanic courts
    - Appear in a satanic crystal ball
    - Appear before any deity

8. Lord Jesus Christ, by Your sacrificial death on the Cross, You swallowed up death in victory. Therefore, based on Your

victory on the Cross on my behalf, I claim my victory over the devil and his companions.

9. As Elijah's sacrifice at the altar brought victory to him over the evil forces of Baal, so shall my sacrifices pave way for my victory, in the name of Jesus Christ.

10. On the day that Jesus sacrificed His life on the Cross, the temple veil rent **(Matthew 27:51)**. So I pray that my sacrifice of prayer shall tear into pieces every garment of reproach over my life, in the name of Jesus Christ.

11. Lord Jesus Christ, help me to learn to embrace sacrifice as a way of life—I pray in the name of Jesus Christ.

12. As Abraham offered Isaac to the Lord, so I offer myself wholly to God, in the name of Jesus Christ.

13. Lord Jesus Christ, let my sacrifices bring me closer to You, in the name of Jesus Christ.

14. Lord Jesus Christ, let my sacrifices win many souls for the Kingdom of Heaven, in the name of Jesus Christ.

15. Lord Jesus Christ, help me to be willing to commit out-of-the-ordinary, intentional acts of selfless sacrifice, never to be deterred by the price I have to pay—in the name of Jesus Christ.

16. Lord Jesus Christ, grant me the grace to share with others what I want to keep for myself, in the name of Jesus Christ.

17. I decree that *my sacrifice of prayer* **"shall be kept burning; it shall not go out" (Leviticus 6:12),** in the name of Jesus Christ.

18. I decree that my Altar of prayer shall not become powerless, in the name of Jesus Christ.

19. I decree that my Altar of prayer shall divert every invisible arrow that is flying in the spiritual realm to hit me, my household or property—in the name of Jesus Christ.

20. *"The [evil] altar also was torn down, and the ashes poured out from the altar, according to the sign that the man of God had given by the word of the Lord"* (1 Kings 13:5).
    a. As Jeroboam's projection against God's Prophet backfired, so shall every satanic projection against me and my loved ones backfire, in the name of Jesus Christ;
    b. I command every evil altar that is used to summon my spirit to their altar or mirror to be arrested, in the name of Jesus Christ;
    c. I command every evil altar that is speaking evil against me to become dumb, in the name of Jesus Christ.

21. The Altar of Jesus on the hills of Calvary speaks healing, deliverance, and victory into my life, in the name of Jesus Christ.

22. Begin to decree the following, in the name of Jesus Christ:
    a. You evil altars raised against me, there shall be no sacrifices or worship on you again!
    b. I decree that every evil altar that is erected within a 200-mile radius from this location is set ablaze.

23. Thank You, Lord Jesus Christ, for accepting my sacrifice of prayers.
    a. I thank You, Lord Jesus Christ, for destroying every evil sacrifice that is meant to harm me and my loved ones;
    b. Thank You, Lord Jesus Christ, for sacrificing Your life on the Cross to give me and the entire humanity freedom.

24. I cover this prayer with the Most Precious Blood of Jesus Christ (7 times).

Chapter 5

The Name Of Jesus Christ

"Therefore God also has highly exalted Him and given Him the name which is above every name, that at the name of Jesus every knee should bow, of those in heaven, and of those on earth, and of those under the earth, and that every tongue should confess that Jesus Christ is Lord, to the glory of God the Father."

(Philippians 2:9-11, NKJV)

[Other suggested Bible passages to read:
Mark 16:17-18, Luke 10:17-20, Mark 9:38-40, Romans 10:13,
Colossians 3:17, Proverbs 18:10].

DAY 10 - Part 1: Reflection

There is unimaginably great Power in the name of Jesus Christ. Praying in the name of Jesus is powerful because when we pray in His name, we pray with His authority. God promises to answer whatever we ask in His name according to His will (John 14:14). We see how powerful the name of Jesus is when used in the casting of demons or when applied directly against the occults and other agents of the devil. Those in the occult and other groups in the kingdom of darkness have no doubt that there is unimaginable Power in the name of Jesus Christ. Think of the name of Jesus as being the key to unlock the Power of God, just as a key is required to unlock the power residing in the engine of a bulldozer, an airplane or a warship.

I once heard the story of an evangelist who was preaching in a territory dominated by Muslims. He wanted to demonstrate to the people in a Church program that there is Power in the name of Jesus Christ and not in any other name. He called to the stage a woman possessed with an evil spirit and a man who clearly had a need for physical healing. Then, in the name of Mohammad, he commanded the evil spirit in the woman to come out. He also commanded the man to be healed in the name of Mohammed but nothing happened in both cases: The woman was not delivered from the evil spirit and the man was not healed from his infirmity. However, when he used the name of Jesus Christ in the prayer, immediately the evil spirits departed from the woman and the man got healed. Waoh! What a great Power in the name of Jesus Christ! Jesus' name is truly *"the name that is above every name"* **(Philippians 2:9)**. All demon spirits, as well as the devil himself, must obey the name of Jesus Christ.

No one can make demons subject to one without the name of Jesus Christ. Demons are overcome and subdued only in the Power of Christ's Holy name—and not in the name of any religious leader, or king, or righteous man, or prophet, or even gods. One day John said to Jesus, *"Teacher, we saw someone driving out demons in your name"* **(Mark 9:38-40)** — not in the name of the gods whose altars they knew. The reason is simple: *"There is salvation in no one else, for there is no other name under heaven given among mortals by which we must be saved"* **(Acts 4:12)**. We profess in the Creed that Jesus Christ came down from heaven *"for us and our salvation."* This truth colors everything about our Savior, Jesus Christ.

There is no power in those other names, and so the devil cannot be subject to us in their names. Look at the lead verse again **(Philippians 2:9-11)**. Do you catch there that the name of Jesus is above every other name? That was why nothing happened on the stage when the minister tried to cast the demons in the name of Mohammed—just as nothing would have happened if any other name other than Jesus was used.

Have you ever noticed that in many secular circles, calling or mentioning the name of Jesus Christ can provoke reactions, although it is acceptable to use other names? Many have gotten attacked by strangers just for mentioning this powerful name. It is quite insulting and demeaning to use the name of Jesus Christ in vain! To take Christ's name in vain is to fail to acknowledge that He is the name that is above all names.

This simple experiment with the name of Jesus Christ versus the name of Mohammed clearly reveals two undeniable truths: (1) That there is incredible Power in the name of Jesus Christ (it is a name of great Power), and (2) The name of Jesus is above every other name. Jesus, Himself, tells us: *"All authority in heaven and on earth has been given to me"* (Matthew 28:18). For this reason, He demonstrated His authority and power over nature and evil, through miracles, healings, and casting out of demons during His earthly ministry. Then, finally, He defeated Satan and his entire kingdom of darkness on the Cross. It is not possible to have successful spiritual warfare without the authority and power of Jesus Christ working in us through the Holy Spirit.

Jesus tells us that in His name shall we cast out the devil (**Mark 16:17**). Jesus is our Deliverer (**1 John 4:4**)! We know for sure *"that at the name of Jesus every knee should bow, of those in heaven, and of those on earth, and of those under the earth"* (**Philippians 2:10, NKJV**). The name of Jesus is the authority of the believer to fight spiritual enemies. It is not our voice that Satan hears and bows, but the authority in the name of Jesus proclaimed with faith. Romans 10:13 clearly states that *"everyone who calls on the name of the Lord [with faith] shall be saved."*

Jesus stripped from Satan and his kingdom the authority given to them over the earth but gave it to His Church (The Body of Christ). The Church has all the power and authority of our Lord Jesus Christ on the earth. It is appropriate to state here that Jesus Christ has given the power of attorney to His Church, authorizing the Church to represent or act on His behalf in the matters or affairs of Heaven. The Church has His authority and the key to this authority is found in the "Name of Jesus Christ." The first century Church actually walked on the power of the name of Jesus Christ. It is unfortunate that the contemporary Church has not fully awakened to this fact yet.

We see the power in the name of Jesus Christ at work as the disciples of the first century Church were healing people and working many miracles in the name of Jesus Christ. The Bible clearly tells us that *"Whatever you do, in word or deed, do everything in the name of the Lord Jesus, giving thanks to God the Father through Him* (Colossians 3:17).

The message is clear: There's great power in the name of Jesus Christ! Before I conclude the writing of this chapter, I wish to share this thrilling story with you. I share this story to motivate you to always pray with the name of Jesus Christ.

A few years ago, a family went out to watch an exciting movie. Unfortunately, right in the middle of the movie, their teenage boy stopped breathing. It was heartbreaking to watch the agonizing cry of a father pleading with his son to start breathing again. He cried out with all his heart, *"David, breathe! David, breathe!!"* But David just laid there breathless. The movie was stopped abruptly as fear gave rise to an atmosphere charged with extreme panic. In the middle of this tension, a man walked right over to where the boy was lying motionless, stooped down, laid his hands on him, and quietly said, *"In the name of Jesus, breathe."* Suddenly, David came to life and began to breathe! Does God answer prayers in the name of Jesus Christ? Yes!

I wish to repeat myself: There is power in the name of Jesus Christ. I hope this story revolutionizes your faith and gives you great boldness and confidence in the power that is in the name of Jesus Christ. You will tap into heaven's power and change earth with your prayers when you pray in the name of Jesus Christ. *"The name of the Lord is a strong tower; the righteous run into it and are safe"* **(Proverbs 18:10)**. It is time to hear your own story!

LET US PRAY!
1. Reflect on how this reflection on *"The Name of Jesus Christ"* ministers to you.

2. Pray and ask God for the forgiveness of your sins using **Psalm 51.**

3. Put on the full armor of God by praying *"The Warrior's Prayer"* (see page 18).

4. Pray *"The Act of Spiritual Communion"* prayer (see page 19).

5. Pray Psalm 83 (a prayer to abort the conspiracy of the enemies).

6. Make your requests in the name of Jesus Christ:
    a. O, Jesus Christ, Your Word says, *"Ask and you shall receive, seek and you shall find, knock and it shall be opened"* **(Matthew 7:7)**. Therefore, I knock, I seek, and I ask that my prayer requests be granted according to Your Most Holy will (*make your request*);
    b. O, Jesus Christ, Your Word says, *"All that you ask of the Father in My Name, He will grant you"* **(John 16:23)**. Therefore, I humbly and urgently ask Your Father in Your name that my prayer requests be granted according to Your Most Holy will (*make your request*);
    c. O, Jesus Christ, Your Word says, *"Heaven and earth shall pass away but My Word shall not pass away"* **(Matthew 24:35)**.

Therefore, I feel confident that my prayer will be granted as Your Word over my life shall come to pass according to Your Most Holy will (*make your request*).

7. Thank You Lord Jesus Christ for answering my prayers. I cover this prayer with the Most Precious Blood of Jesus Christ (7 times).

DAY 11 - Part 2: Warfare Prayers

Note:

- The name of Jesus Christ is mighty! Walk in the power of that great Name!

- It is fitting and very proper to pray in the "Name of Jesus Christ."

- The devil is already defeated—but you have to enforce your victory!

1. Praise and worship God as the Holy Spirit leads you.

2. Pray for the forgiveness of sins.
   a. Examination of Conscience (*if guilty of any of the following, ask God for mercy and forgiveness*):
      i. Do I take the Lord's Name in vain (**Exodus 20:7**)?
      ii. Do I honor any deity other than the Living God?
      iii. Do I get angry when the name of Jesus Christ is mentioned?
      iv. Do I misrepresent the character of Jesus Christ by my actions?
      v. Do I submit myself fully to the Lordship of Jesus Christ?
      vi. Do I give Jesus all honor, praise, and worship?

      vii. Do I ridicule or attack those who identify themselves as followers of Christ?

   b. In the name of the Lord Jesus Christ, I now renounce, break and loose myself, my family, and my bloodline from any bondage due to covenants with deities (or with anything that does not bring honor to the authority of Jesus Christ).

   c. Pray **Psalm 51** to ask God for the forgiveness of your sins.

3. Put on the full armor of God by praying *"The Warrior's Prayer"* (see page 18).

4. Pray *"The Act of Spiritual Communion"* prayer (see page 19).

5. I cover myself and my household, and the environment of this prayer with the Most Precious Blood of Jesus Christ—in the name of Jesus Christ (7 times).

6. Heavenly Father, through this prayer, I come to You in the name of Your Son, Lord Jesus Christ. In His name, I ask You to accept my prayers.

7. I submit myself to Jesus Christ and I stand against all of Satan's influences, in the name of Jesus Christ.

8. Satan, I command you, in the name of the Lord Jesus Christ, to leave my presence with all your demons, and I bring the Blood of the Lord Jesus Christ between us.

9. I reject out of my life all the whispers, accusations, and the temptations of the devil, in the name of Jesus Christ.

10. Lord Jesus Christ, Your Word says in **Mark 16:17** that *"In my name shall they cast out devils."*

   a. Therefore, I exercise authority over every rebel spirits to obey my voice and be cast to the abyss, in the name of

Jesus Christ;

   b. I confess that my body is the temple of the Holy Spirit, redeemed, cleansed, and sanctified by the Blood of Jesus Christ. Therefore:

      i. Satan has no place in me, and has no power over me;

      ii. I command every unclean spirit in me (or any member of my family) to depart now to the abyss, in the name of Jesus Christ.

11. *"But to all who received Him, who believed in His name, He gave [the] power to become children of God"* (John 1:12).

   a. Lord Jesus Christ, I believe in Your name;

   b. Lord Jesus Christ, I thank You for giving me the power to be called a child of God.

12. Thank You, Heavenly Father, for the gift of Your Son, Lord Jesus Christ, whose name opens heaven for us. Thank You, Father, for answering us when we pray to You in His Name.

   a. Thank You, Lord Jesus Christ, for accepting my prayers;

   b. I thank You, Lord Jesus Christ, for the power of Your name made available for all believers to use in fighting the kingdom of darkness;

   c. Thank You, Lord Jesus Christ, for the grace to tap into heaven's power (and change earth) with our prayers when we pray in Your Mighty Name.

13. I cover this prayer with the Most Precious Blood of Jesus Christ (7 times).

Chapter 6

The Word Of God

"The sword of the Spirit...is the Word of God"
(Ephesians 6:17)

"For the Word of God is living and active, sharper than any two-edged sword, piercing to the division of soul and of spirit, of joints and of marrow, and discerning the thoughts and intentions of the heart."
(Hebrews 4:12)

"Very truly, I tell you, anyone who hears my Word and believes him who sent me has eternal life, and does not come under judgment, but has passed from death to life."
(John 5:24)

[Other suggested Bible passages to read:
Joshua 1:7-18, 1 Thessalonians 2:13, 1 Peter 1:25,
1 Timothy 4:13-15, 2 Timothy 3:15-17, James 1:21-25,
Isaiah 55:11, Isaiah 34:16, Psalm 119:97-99].

DAY 12 - Part 1: Reflection

What did God use to create the world? The spoken Word! How did God redeem the world? The Word! *"And the Word became flesh and lived among us"* (John 1:14). Which armor of God did Jesus use in the desert when Satan came to tempt Him? The

Word! Three times Jesus threw the Word to the devil, saying *"It is written"* (**Matthew 4: 4**). Jesus quoted the Word of God written in the Scripture. He overcame every temptation by one weapon — the Word of God. No wonder the Centurion told Jesus saying, ***"Lord, I am not worthy to have You come under my roof; but only speak the Word, and my servant will be healed" (Matthew 8:8)***. It was His spoken Word that healed the Centurion's servant.

If Jesus would use this weapon, then we should! He used it because He knows that the Word of God is all-powerful. Even Satan knows the overwhelming power of the Word of God. He fears it and would do everything possible to make you ignorant of the Word.

The Word of God is very powerful!

I recently visited a close friend in the hospital whose sickness defied all medical solution. It was a very rare disease and its mortality rate is very high. Not much was known about this disease by his doctors. Within a few days, he deteriorated to a very bad shape—so bad that I'd not recognize him. It was in the midst of this hopeless situation that Jesus spoke to my friend saying, "I will turn things around!" Today, as I write this chapter, he is a free man, going about his business. Doctors are amazed at his recovery! My friend encountered the spoken Word of Jesus Christ. All you need for the arrest of every storm in your life is a Word from Jesus Christ. By His spoken Word, demons were cast out, chains of bondage broken, and death overcome.

"I am He" (**John 18:5**). This was the Word of Jesus to the band of soldiers sent to arrest Him in the garden of Gethsemane. This Word was so powerful that ***"When Jesus said, 'I am He,' they drew back and fell to the ground" (John 18:6)***. Please, take note that these men who turned around and fell to the ground when Jesus spoke His Word were soldiers, men trained to be strong and tough. They were not civilians! Someone whose spoken Word carries a force

that would, on its own, knock soldiers to the ground must possess unimaginable Power! His Word must carry a tremendous force. That Man is Jesus! His Word carries Power!

We live in a world that wants to see power. Unfortunately, the world searches for power in the wrong places. As a result, many have dabbled into the occult and witchcraft in search of power. We are torn apart by the idols we have erected and preferred over God. The power of Tech in our contemporary time seems to shift our minds further away from God. We digress from God and from the primitive culture of the first century Christianity who lived by the power of God's Word (the Gospel).

We are the age with more Bibles than any other time in human history, yet we are the most detached from the Bible in all history. The result is that we have become a society falling through the cracks of godlessness into an empty religiosity. I jokingly would say that the tech-savvy people of our contemporary world might feel deterred from the Bible because they think it is old and there are no sounds and no nifty graphics in it, yet its Truths are always new and its power eternally tremendous!

The truth is that there's more power in God's Word than in any cutting-edge Tech our world will ever know. And no matter how high-tech this world gets, we shall never experience a more potent power than the Word of God. We know that *"the Gospel came to you not in Word only, but also in power"* (1 Thessalonians 1:5). **Romans 1:16** says, *"It is the power of God for salvation to everyone who has faith."*

The Word of God carries with it an incredible force to attack the spiritual forces fighting us *"for the Kingdom of God is...in power"* (1 Corinthians 4:20)! We know of this truth in **Jeremiah 23:29** as the Lord asks: *"Is not My Word like fire...and like a hammer which shatters a rock?"*

More so, obedience to the Word of God is also a powerful weapon to overcome the evil forces.. The Word of God is powerful (Hebrews 4:12)! Most believers can quote **Hebrews 4:12** offhand with some accuracy (see the chapter's lead Scripture), but there are not so many who are skillful at using the Word in spiritual battle. Living by God's Word is to live a victorious Christian life. Therefore, God commands us to *"diligently observe the Word"* **(Deuteronomy 29:9)**. The spiritual tyrants have no chance against us in battles if we would only step out in faith and fight them with *"the sword of the Spirit, the Word of God"* **(Ephesians 6:17)**.

From the very mouth of Jesus Christ, we learn that we should *"live by ... every Word that comes from the mouth of God"* **(Matthew 4:4)**. Why was Ezekiel a powerful prophet of God? Simple: He was a man of the Word— Fifty times in the Book of Ezekiel, Prophet Ezekiel reported *"The Word of the Lord came to me"* **(Ezekiel 13:1)**. You can't have the Word without having its power. The Word of God that Ezekiel spoke changed the destiny of the dry bones. It is the Word of God sent out that *"healed them, and delivered them from destruction"* **(Psalm 107:20)**.

Likewise, it is the Word of God from your mouth (spoken with faith) that propels swords of fire straight into the hearts of the devil and his allies. The Bible—the written Word of God (the Logos)— was given to us to discover our inheritance and to harvest the power therein. The power in the written Word is made manifest in the Spoken Word (the Rhema). This spoken Word of God holds creative power. By it, God created the world. Also by it, you reshape your world and recover your lost inheritance!

The Word of God is that spiritual sword *"sharper than any two-edged sword, piercing"* and cutting through the air like a flaming rocket **(Hebrews 4:12, Ephesians 6:17)**. Also our hearts are pierced by His Words as they cut directly to the core of who we are with its burning fire. Were not the hearts of the disciples burning within them while He spoke His Word to them on their way to Emmaus **(Luke 24:32)**?

When we understand the power in the Word of God, we shall send them out like missiles of fire to destroy every Goliath attacking us. Don't doubt the power of the Word of God! The Word of God is the Power of God. For this reason, demonic spirits react to the Word of God. They also fear people who are rooted in the Word of God because such people carry the fire in the Word (the Word of God is fire!).

The enemy knows that if he can get you to lose hope in what the Word of God says concerning the circumstances you are facing, then he has gotten you. Make a quality decision today to trust the integrity of God's Word and believe it with all your heart. Continue to confess what the Word of God says in the Scriptures concerning the situation you are going through, and not what the circumstance is dictating to you.

You are spiritually healthy and powerful to the extent of the Word of God you have in you. Just as we aim to feed our bodies with healthy food, the Word of God is like a meal for our spirit. Would you not agree with me that one week without the Word makes you weak?

Therefore, it is vital to have a constant diet of the Word of God by prayerfully meditating on His Word for our spiritual vitality. The Bible contains all the *"spiritual nutrients"* we need for a healthy soul. Prophet Jeremiah understood this and he wrote: **"Your words were found, and I ate them"** (Jeremiah 15:16).

We have to open the Bible before we can eat and digest the Word therein. Slow, thoughtful absorption of the Word of God with a quiet reflection on its implications is high in nutrition. His Word provides all the ingredients and nourishment that we need in order to grow spiritually and to live life spiritually healthy, such as:

1. The Word of God is the tablets of spiritual vitamins (a preventive medicine that keeps us from sin)

2. The Word of God sanctifies our hearts **(John 17:17)**

3. The Word of God provides spiritual strength (the food of God's champions)

4. The Word of God connects our souls to God

5. The Word of God is the mind's food that makes us wise and discerning

6. The Word of God is the revealer of the spiritual conditions of our hearts

There really isn't a substitute for assimilating the Word into our lives daily.

LET US PRAY!
1. Reflect on how this reflection on *"The Word of God"* ministers to you.

2. Pray and ask God for the forgiveness of your sins using **Psalm 51.**

3. Put on the full armor of God by praying *"The Warrior's Prayer"* (see page 18).

4. Pray *"The Act of Spiritual Communion"* prayer (see page 19).

5. Pray **Psalm 119:89-96** (a prayer to delight in God's Word).

6. Lord Jesus Christ, help me to..... (*pick from the following list*), in the name of Jesus Christ:

   • Walk in Your Word **(Jeremiah 7:23)**
   • Live by Your Word

- Obey Your Word (Jeremiah 7:23)
- Stand by Your Word
- Dress up with Your Word
- Seek Your Word (Amos 8:12)
- Truly understand Your Word
- Carry Your Word in me (Jeremiah 20:9)
- Be set me free by Your Word (John 8:31)
- Walk by Your Word (Psalm 119:105)
- Be healed by Your Word (Psalm 107:20)
- Have a deep thirst for Your Word
- Let Your Word abide in me (John. 15:7)
- Always keep Your Word on my lips (Joshua 1:8)
- Meditate on Your Word daily (Joshua 1:8)
- Hear Your Word and do what it says
- Overcome the evil one (1 John 2:14)

7. I take up the shield of faith and the sword of the Spirit (the Word of God) to battle in the spiritual realm against all the spiritual enemies of my life—I pray in the name of Jesus Christ.

8. *"He sent out His Word and healed them, snatching them from the door of death"* (Psalm 107:20, NLT). Make the following prayers in the name of Jesus Christ:
   a. God's Word is healing me (Psalm 107:20);
   b. God's Word is cleansing me (Ephesians 5:26);
   c. God's Word is melting whatever the enemy has put in me (Psalm 147:18);
   d. God's Word is breaking every limitation in my life (Jeremiah 23:29);
   e. God's Word is delivering me from the forces of darkness (Matthew 8:16);
   f. God's Word is overcoming the evil one against my life (I John 2: 14);
   g. God's Word inputs the "spirit and life" in me (John 6:63);
   h. God's Word is setting me free from ignorance, deception, and sin.

9. Lord Jesus Christ, enable me to use Your Word not only to defend me from Satan and his companions but also (pray the following in the name of Jesus Christ):
   a. To claim its promises;
   b. To wield the sword strong against Satan so as to defeat him;
   c. To push them (the devil and his companions) back to forgetfulness;
   d. To take away from him (the devil) every ground that he claims against me;
   e. To win great victories.

10. Thank You Lord Jesus Christ for answering my prayers. I cover this prayer with the Most Precious Blood of Jesus Christ (7 times).

DAY 13 - Part 2: Warfare Prayers

Note:
- God honors His Word whenever it is spoken, and great is the power thereof. The power of God's Word is immeasurable!

- At the heart of our Christian life is the Meal of the Word and the Eucharist.

- Jesus proclaims in His Word that He is the Truth **(John 14:6)**. Many can say, *"I have taught you the truth."* Only Jesus Christ can say, I am the Truth. His Word is the Truth!

1. Praise and worship God as the Holy Spirit leads you.

2. Pray for the forgiveness of your sins: ***"That He might sanctify and cleanse her with the washing of water by the Word"*** **(Ephesians 5:26, NKJV)**. Ask God to sanctify you by His Word **(John 17:17)**.
   a. Examination of Conscience *(if guilty of any of the following,*

ask God for mercy and forgiveness):
  i. Do I believe that the Bible is the written Word of God?
  ii. Do I believe God's Word and receive it as if my life depended on it?
  iii. Do I nourish my faith with prayerful reflections on the Word of God?
  iv. Do I believe that God's Word is trustworthy and infallible?
  v. Do I believe and live in the truth and power of God's Word?
  vi. Do I meditate upon God's Word?
  vii. Do I strive to open my heart and mind to God's Truth?
  viii. Do I allow other voices to distract me from listening to God?

  b. Lord Jesus Christ, forgive and cleanse me from the sin of neglecting Your Word;

  c. Lord Jesus Christ, let Your Word free me from my own sinful blindness, stubborn pride, and ignorance;

  d. Pray **Psalm 51** to ask God for the forgiveness of your sins.

3. Put on the full armor of God by praying *"The Warrior's Prayer"* (see page 18).

4. Pray *"The Act of Spiritual Communion"* prayer (see page 19).

5. I cover myself and my household, and the environment of this prayer with the Most Precious Blood of Jesus Christ—in the name of Jesus Christ (7 times).

6. Lord Jesus Christ *(pray the following in the name of Jesus Christ):*
  a. Let Your Word enter into my heart;
  b. Make my heart burn within me with Your Word;
  c. Grant me the grace to comprehend the deeper meaning of Your Word;

d. In Your Word I find life, truth, and freedom;

e. May Your Word daily dwell in the sanctuary of my heart;

f. May I listen to Your Word attentively and obey it joyfully;

g. May I never doubt Your life-giving Word;

h. Nourish me with Your life-giving Word.

i. May I be rooted and built up in Your Word;

j. Sanctify my heart by Your Word **(John 17:17)**;

k. Grant that I may be a doer of Your Word;

l. Grant me a great love for Your Word;

m. I choose to live my life in the light of God's Word;

n. Write Your Word in my heart;

o. I reject whatever is false and contrary to Your Word;

p. Help me to draw nearer to Your Word;

q. Help me to trust in Your life-giving Word;

7. Ask the Holy Spirit to take the nutrients of God's Word and build you up from the inside out. Make the following prayers in the name of Jesus Christ:

a. Ask Him to reveal God to You in the Scripture;

b. Ask Him to help you commit to reading the Bible every day;

c. Ask Him for a healthier relationship with God through His Word.

8. Holy Spirit, let nothing stand in the way of my hearing, listening to and following God's Word, in the name of Jesus Christ.

9. Holy Spirit, let God's Word pierce my heart and keep it on fire for Jesus, in the name of Jesus Christ.

10. Lord Jesus Christ, let Your Word be on my lips and in my heart that I may walk in the freedom of Your everlasting love, truth, and goodness, in the name of Jesus Christ.

11. Jesus says, *"Very truly, I tell you, whoever keeps My Word will never see death"* (John 8:51). Holy Spirit, help me (pray in the name of Jesus Christ):
    a. To believe in the Word of Jesus Christ and to obey it with all my heart, mind, and strength;
    b. To think, live and act in the knowledge of God's Word;
    c. To hear Your voice, and not harden my heart to that which You ask of me;
    d. *"Never to see [eternal] death"* (John 8:51).

12. Lord Jesus Christ, remove whatever closes my mind (and the minds of people) to Your Word, in the name of Jesus Christ. Pray the following in the name of Jesus Christ:
    a. May I hear no other voices but Yours!
    b. May Your Word strengthen and empower me!

13. Thank You, Lord Jesus Christ, for:
    a. The power of Your Word that causes the devil and his cohorts to retreat from me;
    b. Blessing me with Your Word;
    c. Nourishing and strengthening my life with Your Word.

14. I cover this prayer with the Most Precious Blood of Jesus Christ (7 times).

Chapter 7

The Fire Of God

"Know then today that the Lord your God is the One who crosses over before you as a devouring fire; He will defeat them and subdue them before you, so that you may dispossess and destroy them quickly, as the Lord has promised you."

(Deuteronomy 9:3)

[Other suggested Bible passages to read:
Matthew 3:10-12, Luke 12:49, Deuteronomy 4:23-25,
Isaiah 30:27-30, 2 Thessalonians 1:7,
Exodus 19:18, Exodus 24:17].

DAY 14 - Part 1: Reflection

I was thrilled during my high school Physics class to observe that a piece of paper can be set aflame by focusing the sun's rays on it for a period of time through a magnifying glass. I held the magnifying glass over the paper until the paper began to smoke and then caught fire. Although lighting a fire with a magnifying glass takes much more time than using a lighter or a match, yet the excitement I had with this experiment would drive me to be patient till the blazing sun begins to set my paper on fire!

Similarly, we can spiritually set our hearts aflame by exposing ourselves to His Presence: God's Light through His Word (the

Scriptures) and by our communion with Him through our prayers. The men on their way to Emmaus confessed: *"Were not our hearts burning within us while He was talking to us on the road [extended exposure to His Light], while He was opening the Scriptures [the Word] to us?* (Luke 24:32).

God is Fire: Not only that *"Our God is a consuming Fire"* (Hebrews 12:29), but our God is also a Wall of Fire (Zechariah 2:5). He is the Fire that consumes fire! His Fire is in us when we have Him in us. Jesus wishes His Fire *"were already kindled"* in us (Luke 12:49)! When you are a flaming fire, you are very hot and too dangerous for the devil to handle. Your prayer carries the fire of God.

Feed the flames of God in you with the Word of God. We have been commissioned to light the fire of prayer! Although the Fire of God warms our spirit up and sets our hearts on fire, yet it is also a weapon as it burns up and destroys everything that is evil in and around us.

Think of a candle. Its fire drives away darkness and, with the same fire, consumes its wax. In a similar way, the fire of God in us does not only dispel the agents of darkness from us, it also melts all that *"brings forth...evil"* (Luke 6:45). Deuteronomy 9:3 says, *"Know then today that the Lord your God is the One who crosses over before you as a devouring fire; He will defeat them and subdue them before you, so that you may dispossess and destroy them quickly, as the Lord has promised you."*

God's Fire is an all-purpose weapon that consumes every habitation of cruelty militating against you. God expects you to use this fire to set ablaze the enemies and destroy them (Obadiah 1:18). You fuel your fire with God's Word so that the flames can shoot out to consume the spiritual enemies (Psalm 39:3-4). His Word is like a fire (Jeremiah 20:9). God is now saying to you: *"I am now making My Words in your mouth a fire"* (Jeremiah 5:14).

The enemy has no chance against this awesome and powerful weapon. How can the kingdom of darkness stand against the God from Whose feet *"burning coals went forth"* (Habakkuk 3:5, AKJV), Whose *"Tongue is like a devouring fire"* (Isaiah 30:27), and *"His breath is like an overflowing stream that reaches up to the neck—to sift the nations with the sieve of destruction"* (Isaiah 30:28)? Psalm 97:3 says, *"Fire goes before Him, and consumes His adversaries on every side."* In another occasion, *"The Lord God was calling for a shower of fire, and it devoured the great deep and was eating up the land"* (Amos 7:4). No enemy can stand the engulfing Fire of our God. The Scripture says: *"And fire came down from heaven and consumed them"* (Revelation 20:9).

Our God is the Fire that makes His people fire! During deliverance sessions, this Fire of God manifests like a flow of anointing shooting out as rays of fire from the fingertips, eyes, and even the entire body of the deliverance minister. We know that this is true when God opens our eyes to see in the spirit. We also know it is true because the Scripture says so in **Hebrews 1:7**—*"He makes ... his servants flames of fire."*

The Fire of God emanating from His servants routs unclean spirits, forcing them to flee from someone being delivered. Most times, as the spirits leave, you may notice people reacting to the anointing with manifestations of falling and rolling violently on the floor. Sometimes, there is a violent kicking, screaming, foaming in the mouth or even outright fight against the minister (please, note that not all "falling on the ground" during prayer is a demonic manifestation).

Through Christ, with Christ, and in Christ, our lives become earth-shaking instruments of fire to drive out the tyrant spirits from our lives as the current of His anointing is released. Like Elijah, who in **2 Kings 1:9-15** called down the fire of God to consume the two bands of fifty men that king Ahaziah sent unto him, you can also call on this fire weapon to consume satanic hordes.

It's time to call down fire from heaven. It's time to invoke God's fire of judgment on the wicked works of darkness. It's time to demand your deliverance and refuse nothing else until you are free. It's time to challenge all prophets of Baal against your life and show them that your God is a consuming Fire!

LET US PRAY!
1. Reflect on how this reflection on *"The Fire of God"* ministers to you.

2. Pray and ask God for the forgiveness of your sins using **Psalm 51.**

3. Put on the full armor of God by praying *"The Warrior's Prayer"* (see page 18).

4. Pray *"The Act of Spiritual Communion"* prayer (see page 19).

5. Pray **Psalm 20** (a prayer for victory).

6. Heavenly Father, I ask You, in the name of Your Son Jesus Christ, to make me a flame of fire according to Your Word in **Hebrews 1:7.**

7. Lord Jesus Christ, release Your coals of fire to destroy the spiritual forces of darkness coming after my life **(Psalm 18:13)**, in the name of Jesus Christ.

8. Holy Spirit, I confess with my mouth that Your Fire burns..... (*pick from the following list*), in the name of Jesus Christ.
    - In my eyes
    - In my feet
    - On my skin
    - In my belly
    - In my heart
    - In my tongue
    - In my hands
    - In my mouth
    - Around me

9. Thank You Lord Jesus Christ for answering my prayers. I cover this prayer with the Most Precious Blood of Jesus Christ (7 times).

DAY 15 - Part 2: Warfare Prayers

Note:

- Before applying the Fire of God (or any of the other weapons), always ensure that every legal ground that gives Satan the legal rights to attack you is dealt with. What creates legal grounds for Satan are most often, unconfessed sins and unbroken demonic covenants.

1. Praise and worship God as the Holy Spirit leads you.

2. Pray for the forgiveness of sins (pray **Psalm 51**). Holy Spirit:
    a. Let Your Fire consume every seed of stubbornness and disobedience in me;
    b. By Your Fire, draw me into repentance and a new fervent walk with God.

3. Put on the full armor of God by praying *"The Warrior's Prayer"* (see page 18).

4. Pray *"The Act of Spiritual Communion"* prayer (see page 19).

5. I cover myself and my household, and the environment of this prayer with the Most Precious Blood of Jesus Christ—in the name of Jesus Christ (7 times).

6. Holy Spirit, I come before You today for a new baptism. Make the following prayers in the name of Jesus Christ:
    a. I ask for the Baptism of the Holy Spirit:
        i.   In your life;
        ii. In the life of God's ministers;
        iii. In the global Church.
    b. Let every chaff in me be burned up and destroyed from today onwards;
    c. May every thought, idea, and attitude in me which does

not bear the right fruits be hewn down and cast into fire according to **Matthew 3:10;**

7. Begin to confess the following in the name of Jesus Christ:
    a. I have received a tongue of Fire;
    b. The words of my mouth carry Fire;
    c. I am a minister of Fire **(Hebrews 1:7);**
    d. Before me fire devours, behind me a flame blazes **(Joel 2:3);**
    e. I am a charging fire that cannot be quenched **(Leviticus 6:13);**
    f. I am delivered by God's Fire **(Psalm 18:13);**
    g. The Fire of God protects and covers me **(Exodus 14:24);**
    h. The Fire of God is released into my family;
    i. My life is purified by the Fire of God **(Malachi 3:2);**
    j. I am constantly on fire for Jesus Christ;
    k. The Fire of God surrounds me, my family, and my belongings;
    l. The Fire of God melts every yoke in my life;
    m. Like the wise virgins, I carry a well-trimmed lamp with extra oil to sustain my fire **(Matthew 25:1-4);**
    n. The Fire of God in me can never be put out by the dusts of life. Every day of my life, the Fire of God in me is renewed anew;
    o. The Fire of God burns up all the wicked spirits at work in the city I live in;
    p. The glory of God is all over me like a burning Fire;
    q. Every obstacle on my way is as stubble as God's Fire burns them;
    r. No spiritual tyrant fighting me and my family shall escape the flaming swords of God's Angels;
    s. All flesh sees the Fire of God released unto my life;
    t. Demons are exposed and cast out of my life (and the lives of my family members) as the Fire of God burns;
    u. The Holy Spirit inflames my heart with His merciful love;
    v. As the Fire of the Holy Spirit, everything that is not in

THE FIRE OF GOD

accordance with God's will for my life is removed;

w. May I always seek to love You above all else and follow You wherever You wish to lead me;

x. Like a wood burnt to ashes, all evil deposits in me are now *"ashes under the soles of [my] feet"* (Malachi 4.3);

y. The Fire of God destroys every evil arrow projected at me;

z. The Fire of God exposes every evil spirit concealing their identities to attack me.

8. Holy Spirit, bring Your Fire upon the earth for revival and purification in the Body of Christ, in the name of Jesus Christ.

9. Lord Jesus Christ, grant me total deliverance through this prayer, in the name of Jesus Christ. Lord Jesus Christ:

a. Rain fire, brimstone, and tempest upon the kingdoms of Satan;

b. I use the Word of God as a Fire, a hammer, and a two-edged sword to destroy the wicked, in the name of Jesus Christ;

c. Let Your Fire bring forth healing upon the sick.

10. Matthew 7:7 says *"Ask, and it will be given you."* Therefore:

a. Ask the Holy Spirit to place a ring of His Fire around your life and family;

b. Ask the Fire of God to move in you;

c. Ask the Fire of God to purify you so that you may come forth like pure gold.

11. I release the Fire of God to destroy the power of all..... (*pick from the following list*) meant to harm me—in the name of Jesus Christ.

- Curses
- Spells
- Incantations
- Arrows of death
- Magic
- Charms
- Sorcery
- Voodoo
- Blood sacrifices
- Evil projections
- Witchcraft operations

12. O Lord Jesus, You are the God who answers by Fire **(1 Kings 18:24)**. Therefore, answer me by Fire, in the name of Jesus Christ.

13. Holy Spirit, baptize me with Your Fire **(Luke 3:16)**. Your Fire, O LORD, is in my hands heals the sick and cast out the devils, in the name of Jesus Christ.

14. Thank You, Lord Jesus Christ, for not only making me a fire but also for delivering me by Fire, in the name of Jesus Christ.

15. I cover this prayer with the Most Precious Blood of Jesus Christ (7 times)

Chapter 8

The Power of the Holy Spirit

"But you will receive power when the Holy Spirit comes on you, and you will be my witnesses in Jerusalem, and in all Judea and Samaria, and to the ends of the earth."
(Acts 1:8)

"The Spirit helps us in our weakness. For we do not know what to pray for as we ought, but the Spirit Himself intercedes for us with groanings too deep for words."
(Romans 8:26)

[Other suggested Bible passages to read:
Acts 2, Romans 8:26-27, Matthew 3:16-17,
Luke 4:14-22, Ezekiel 47:1-12].

DAY 16 - Part 1: Reflection

A soldier needs to stay in contact with command headquarters and have at his disposal, a constant source of supply of ammunition and security intelligence. Without a constant source of supply of weapons and a system of communication in place, a soldier is destined for a defeat. Thank God we have the Holy Spirit who keeps us in constant communication with the Kingdom of God for the supply of every weapon and Divine Intelligence we need in order to defeat the kingdom of darkness.

The Kingdom of God operates with the Power of the Holy Spirit. He was the Power that raised Lazarus from the dead, parted the sea, broke open prison doors, and caused the lame to walk. He is the same Power still at work within us today. The Holy Spirit's Power is totally sufficient to win spiritual battles against our own fleshly desires and the wiles of the devil and his kingdom.

Victory over the enemy gets accomplished not by our power or by our might, but by the power of the Holy Spirit (**Zechariah 4:6**). The Holy Spirit enables us to do what we, otherwise, couldn't do. He helps us in our weakness (**Romans 8:26**), and enables us to grow in spiritual freedom—freedom from doubt, fear, and from satanic slavery. It is through the Power of the Holy Spirit that we can destroy the power of the enemy and protect all that God has given to us.

The Holy Spirit helps us equip ourselves with all of the spiritual weapons of war. He helps us to fight the good fight of faith. He equips us to live with courage in a dark world. We need the empowerment of the Holy Spirit for the spiritual battle that only He can offer. He is the Vanquisher of rebel spirits! It is, therefore, important to ask the Holy Spirit not only to strengthen us in battle times but to fortify every aspect of our spiritual armament so we don't become vulnerable in any area.

As we learn to tap into the Power of the Holy Spirit, we begin to experience victory in our lives! God fills us with strength, wisdom, and discernment through His own Spirit to stay strong in a spiritual battle. He never leaves us to fend for ourselves and fight with our own strength. He also gives us the strength to persevere in our spiritual journey and the power to resist the devil's deceptions. The ministry of the Holy Spirit helps us to effectively conduct spiritual warfare.

Each and every spiritual battle we experience is completely unique and different from one another, however similar they may seem to be. No two battle situations are ever alike. This is why we totally need to be guided and led by the Holy Spirit who knows how to handle each one of these spiritual battle situations. Victory belongs to us when we follow the Holy Spirit's battle plan! We make mistakes when we do not involve the Holy Spirit in our warfare operations. Take for instance, in **Joshua 9:1-27,** the Lord was not consulted by Joshua and the elders of Israel in dealing with the Gibeonites. As a result, they made a mistake. They were deceived by their physical senses. At the end, they regretted their decision.

LET US PRAY!

1. Reflect on how this reflection on *"The Power of the Holy Spirit"* ministers to you.

2. Pray and ask God for the forgiveness of your sins using **Psalm 51.**

3. Put on the full armor of God by praying *"The Warrior's Prayer"* (see page 18).

4. Pray *"The Act of Spiritual Communion"* prayer (see page 19).

5. Pray **Psalm 42** (a prayer for longing for God and seeking His help in distress).

6. **Prayer of Act of Consecration to the Holy Spirit:** *"On my knees before the great multitude of heavenly witnesses, I offer myself, soul and body to You, Eternal Spirit of God. I adore the brightness of Your purity, the unerring keenness of Your justice, and the might of Your love. You are the Strength and Light of my soul. In You, I live and move and am. I desire never to grieve You by unfaithfulness to grace and I pray with all my heart to be kept from the smallest sin against You. Mercifully guard my every thought and grant that I may always watch for Your light, and listen to Your voice, and follow Your gracious inspirations. I cling to You and give myself to You and ask You, by Your compassion to watch over me in my weakness. Holding the pierced Feet of Jesus and looking at His Five*

Wounds, and trusting in His Precious Blood and adoring His opened Side and stricken Heart, I implore You, Adorable Spirit, Helper of my infirmity, to keep me in Your grace that I may never sin against You. Give me grace, O Holy Spirit, Spirit of the Father and the Son to say to You always and everywhere, 'Speak Lord for Your servant heareth.' Amen." —Unknown Author.

7. **Prayer for the Seven Gifts of the Holy Spirit:** *"O Lord Jesus Christ, Who, before ascending into heaven, did promise to send the Holy Spirit to finish Your work in the souls of Your Apostles and Disciples, deign to grant the same Holy Spirit to me that He may perfect in my soul, the work of Your grace and Your love. Grant me the Spirit of Wisdom that I may despise the perishable things of this world and aspire only after the things that are eternal, the Spirit of Understanding to enlighten my mind with the light of Your divine truth, the Spirit of Counsel that I may ever choose the surest way of pleasing God and gaining heaven, the Spirit of Fortitude that I may bear my cross with You and that I may overcome with courage all the obstacles that oppose my salvation, the Spirit of Knowledge that I may know God and know myself and grow perfect in the science of the Saints, the Spirit of Piety that I may find the service of God sweet and amiable, and the Spirit of Fear that I may be filled with a loving reverence towards God and may dread in any way to displease Him. Mark me, dear Lord, with the sign of Your true disciples and animate me in all things with Your Spirit. Amen"* —Unknown Author.

8. Ask the fire of the Holy Spirit to purify and heal every part of your body including your five senses: touch, sight, hearing, smell, and taste.

9. Heavenly Father, may I have an ever-deeper bonding with You and Your Son, Jesus Christ, through the Holy Spirit, in the name of Jesus Christ.

10. Holy Spirit, may Your light shine through me that others may find new life and joy in You, in the name of Jesus Christ.

11. Make the following healing Prayers (praying each in the name of Jesus Christ):

a. Holy Spirit, let Your healing Fire burn away every sickness in my life;
b. Holy Spirit, with Your Fire, perform Your surgical operation in my life;
c. Holy Spirit, Yoke-breaker, break every yoke in my life;
d. Holy Spirit, with Your Fire, liberate me from all bondage;
e. Holy Spirit, with Your Fire, uproot every spirit of ..... (*pick from the following list*) from me.

- Anger
- Pride
- Lust
- Lie
- Bitterness
- Unforgiveness
- Malice
- Resentment
- Manipulation
- Continue...

12. Holy Spirit, with Your Fire (*pray each prayer in the name of Jesus Christ*):
    a. Destroy every evil altar speaking against my life;
    b. Destroy every eater of my flesh and drinker of my blood;
    c. Make my love for God never to wax cold;
    d. Vanquish every rebel spirit working against me;
    e. Uproot every tree of non-achievement in my bloodline;
    f. Annul every satanic decision or agenda against my life;
    g. Help me to always find the strength I need to love and serve God wholeheartedly.

13. Thank You Lord Jesus Christ for answering my prayers. I cover this prayer with the Most Precious Blood of Jesus Christ (7 times).

DAY 17 - Part 2: Warfare Prayers

Note:
- Have a constant fellowship and relationship with the Holy Spirit.
- As the Israelites followed the pillar of cloud, so must we follow the Holy Spirit.

1. Praise and worship God as the Holy Spirit leads you. Suggested songs:
   a. *"Holy Ghost Fire, Fire fall on me X2...As in the day of the Pentecost, Fire fall on me (X2)"*;
   b. *"All over the world, the Spirit is moving; All over the world, as the prophets said it would be, All over the world, there's a mighty revelation of the glory of the Lord, as the waters cover the sea."*

2. Pray for the forgiveness of your sins.
   a. Examination of Conscience *(if guilty of any of the following, ask God for mercy and forgiveness):*
      i. Do I allow the Holy Spirit to open my mind to understand God's Word?
      ii. Do I hunger for the true and abundant life which God offers through the gift of His Holy Spirit?
      iii. Do I believe in the Ministry of the Holy Spirit?
      iv. Do I believe in The Holy Trinity: God the Father, God the Son, and God the Holy Spirit?
      v. Do I doubt the works or miracles of the Holy Spirit?
   b. Holy Spirit remove everything that is unkind, ungrateful, unloving, and unholy in my life;
   c. Pray **Psalm 51** for the forgiveness of your sins;
   d. Lord Jesus, have mercy on all Your people and heal the divisions in the Body of Christ.

3. Put on the full armor of God by praying *"The Warrior's Prayer"* (see page 18).

4. Pray *"The Act of Spiritual Communion"* prayer (see page 19).

5. Let us pray with St. Augustine: *"Breathe into me, Holy Spirit, that my thoughts may all be holy. Move in me, Holy Spirit, that my work, too, may be holy. Attract my heart, Holy Spirit, that I may love only what is holy. Strengthen me, Holy Spirit, that I may defend all that*

is holy. Protect me, Holy Spirit, that I may always be holy."

6. I ask the Holy Spirit to permeate my mind, heart, body, soul, and spirit, creating a hunger and thirst for God's Holy Word, in the name of Jesus Christ.

7. Holy Spirit, recalibrate the spiritual climate of my life from being lukewarm to being on fire for God, in the name of Jesus Christ.

8. Matthew 7:7 says *"Ask, and it will be given you."* Therefore, Holy Spirit, I ask You to:
   a. Teach me how to pray and make effectively intercessions;
   b. Guide me into a life of holiness;
   c. Make me what God wants me to be;
   d. Help me to love my neighbor when I am tempted to hate;
   e. Help me to live in God's light when I am tempted to live in darkness;
   f. Help me to be obedient to God when I am tempted to go my own way;
   g. Help me to walk in humility when I am tempted to walk in pride;
   h. Help me to live in truth when I am tempted to live in falsehood;
   i. Help us to live together in the bond of unity when I am tempted to live in division;
   j. Speak life into my mortal body;
   k. Release signs, wonders, and miracles into my life by Your Power;
   l. Give me a thirst for God;
   m. Release new outpouring of Your Power. I need Your Fire!
   n. Fill me and transform my heart and mind with Your Spirit;
   o. Make the impossible possible in my life;
   p. Move me to higher spiritual grounds;
   q. Channel Your Divine irrigation to every desert-like place in my life;
   r. Let Your heavenly blessings fall upon my life;
   s. Intervene in the pains I am going through (*mention them*);

t. Trouble everything troubling me;

u. Make me as holy as I should be;

v. Destroy in me all the vices and replace them with their opposites (virtues);

w. Please make me one with You.

9. Holy Spirit, may You have unrestricted and unhindered access into my mind, soul and spirit. I decree that there is no part of my life that is not reserved for You, in the name of Jesus Christ.

10. Holy Spirit, give me the courage to always choose what is Good, True, and Just and to reject whatever is false, foolish, and contrary to Your Holy will—in the name of Jesus Christ.

11. Lord Jesus, fill me with Your Holy Spirit and guide me in Your way of life, truth, and goodness, in the name of Jesus Christ.

12. Holy Spirit, help me to always hunger for God and His Word, in the name of Jesus Christ.

13. I shall drink from the *"Fountain of salvation"* (Isaiah 12:3), in the name of Jesus Christ.

14. The Rivers of the Holy Spirit is flowing out of me (John 7:37-38), in the name of Jesus Christ.

15. Holy Spirit, make Jesus the desire of my heart, in the name of Jesus Christ.

16. Holy Spirit, help me to always live in the joy, peace, and unity with the Holy Trinity, in the name of Jesus Christ.

17. Holy Trinity saturate my family with Your tender, warm, loving presence so that we may recognize and manifest that love in all our relationships, in the name of Jesus Christ.

18. Holy Spirit, give me the power to witness for Jesus Christ with all boldness **(Acts 1:8)**, in the name of Jesus Christ.

19. Pray for the Church. Holy Spirit, I ask You to:
    a. Bring forth revival in the Church again;
    b. Fill everyone in the Church with hunger and thirst for holiness and righteousness;
    c. Dismantle every altar of the occult raised against the Church;
    d. Expose and overthrow all satanic agents in positions of leadership in the Church;
    e. Raise in our time, holy and fearless preachers:
        i. Lord, send more laborers to Your Vineyard;
        ii. Lord, fill Your ministers with a thirst for the salvation of souls;
        iii. Lord, raise great saints in the Church.

20. *"O merciful God, fill our hearts, we pray, with the graces of Your Holy Spirit; with love, joy, peace, patience, gentleness, goodness, faithfulness, humility and self-control. Teach us to love those who hate us; to pray for those who despitefully use us; that we may be the children of your love, our Father, who makes the sun to rise on the evil and the good, and sends rain on the just and on the unjust. In adversity, grant us the grace to be patient; in prosperity keep us humble; may we guard the door of our lips; may we lightly esteem the pleasures of this world and thirst after heavenly things; through Jesus Christ our Lord."* **(Prayer of Anselm, 1033-1109)**.

21. Let us pray with St. Francis of Assisi: *"Lord make me an instrument of your peace. Where there is hatred let me sow love. Where there is an injury, pardon. Where there is doubt, faith. Where there is despair, hope. Where there is darkness, light. And where there is sadness, joy."*

22. *"Come, O Blessed Spirit of Piety, possess my heart. Enkindle therein such a love for God that I may find satisfaction only in His service, and for His sake lovingly submit to all legitimate authority. Amen."*—Unknown Author

23. Holy Spirit, fill up all areas of my life vacated by the forces of evil, in the name of Jesus Christ.

24. Thank You, Lord Jesus Christ, for revealing the immeasurable and unlimited power of God available in me—in the name of Jesus Christ.

25. I cover this prayer with the Most Precious Blood of Jesus Christ (7 times).

Chapter 9

Prayer and Fasting

"But this kind does not go out except by prayer and fasting"

(Matthew 17:21, NASB).

[Other suggested Bible passages to read:
Matthew 18:19-20, Matthew 21:22, Mark 11:24-26,
Matthew 7:7-11, Luke 11:2-4, Luke 11:9-13, John 14:13-14,
John 15:7,16, John 16:23-24, Matthew 5:44,
Luke 6:27-28, Matthew 6:5-15].

DAY 18 - Part 1: Reflection

Fasting and prayer are already known to be very powerful armors in spiritual battles. Prayer is one of the greatest weapons given to the Church, but fasting enhances and boots the power of prayer. Prayer and fasting combined, make up the most critical weapon of spiritual warfare. The two form a huge investment in your weapon store! The power of prayer would even be more intensified— making you spiritually very dangerous— when you are properly armed with these two weapons and blending them with a night-watch prayer (vigil prayer) and some other weapons of warfare! You simply become a dangerous walking fire-explosive!

There are different ranks of evil spirits that correspond to different degrees of life challenges. There are problems that counseling can resolve, and there are problems that prayers alone can solve. However, there are some spiritual issues that without a combination of fasting and prayers, you cannot get victory or results of deliverance **(Matthew 17:21)**. This category of spiritual matters highlights the power of prayer and fasting. On this note, we see that adding a fast to our prayers can make our breakthroughs to come fast. For sure, prayer gives us the answers to life's questions! Prayer is God's solution to any civilization in spiritual crisis, like ours.

For sure, fasting is very important in our fight against spiritual rulers, authorities, cosmic powers of this present darkness and *"against the spiritual forces of evil in the heavenly places"* **(Ephesians 6:12)**. Through fasting and prayers, stubborn enemies can be defeated, overwhelming battles won, supernatural protections released, God's judgments averted and God's mercy received, divine help obtained, and supernatural breakthroughs received. What an awesome weapon is prayer! It is a full suit of armor! I want to encourage you today to take this mighty weapon of warfare and get into battle! You will be amazed by the results that you will begin to harvest.

The enemy hates to see you pray because he knows that the Lord Jesus gets involved in your situation when you pray **(Matthew 18:20)**. **Psalm 107:13-14** says, *"Then they cried to the Lord in their trouble, and he saved them from their distress; He brought them out of darkness and gloom, and broke their bonds asunder."* No matter the power of the devil, God comes down to save us when we begin to pray. The Lord assures us in **Jeremiah 29:12** and **Jeremiah 33:3** that if we call unto Him in prayer, He will hear and answer us.

Prayer is powerful and it has an awesome range when used with fasting. Jesus highlights the need for fasting in dealing with tyrant spirits when He told His disciples who could not cast out a certain demon from a demon-possessed boy saying, *"But this kind does not go out except by prayer and fasting*" (Matthew 17:21, NASB). This deliverance simply highlights how powerful are the prayers of a praying Christian who combines fasting with prayer. For sure, it cannot be argued that combining fasting with prayer and with other spiritual weapons is nothing short of a victory for you!

Since prayer is so important this way, how often, then, should a Christian pray? Just ask Jesus that same question. He would most likely answer you, saying: *"I prayed alone"* (Mathew 14:23, Mark 1:35, Luke 9:18, Luke 22:39-41), *"I prayed in the public"* (John 11:41-42, John 12:27-30), *"I prayed before my meals"* (Matthew 26:26, Mark 8:6, Luke 24:30, John 6:11), *"I prayed before making decisions"* (Luke 6:12-13), *"I prayed before healing"* (Mark 7:34-35), "I prayed after healing" (Luke 5:16), *"I prayed to do My Father's will"* (Matthew 26:36-44). *"I prayed in my anguish until my 'sweat became like great drops of blood falling down on the ground'"* (Luke 22:44). "I prayed for the strength to endure the Cross (Matthew 26:36-46), *"I prayed for the protection of My Apostles and My Church"* (John 17:1-26). *"I prayed for My disciples one by one: I prayed for Peter that His faith may not fail"* (Luke 22:32). *"I pray for you"* (Hebrews 7:25). Jesus continually prayed. For Him, prayer is an ongoing investment!

The life of Jesus Christ was undeniably a life of prayer. We ought to pray always, like Jesus! He is the Eternal Intercessor, who lives to pray for us (Hebrews 7:25)—and His prayers are still being answered.

Prayer is so important for Jesus that He had to teach His disciples how to pray (Luke 11:2-4). It is definitely out of the character of Christ when His disciples or followers (Christians) don't pray. The Bible tells us in 1 Thessalonians 5:17 to *"pray without ceasing."* Even devout Muslims pray five times a day! Too bad that Christians cannot copy this behavior.

By prayer, you can passionately argue your case like Abraham pleading for Sodom when the Angels were heading to the city to destroy it **(Genesis 18:16-33)**. Abraham's intercession saved the family of Lot. How else can we save our family or nation without turning the wheel of prayer? Like a spiritual attorney, you can stand in the gap for your people to save them from perdition. God is actually searching for spiritual attorneys to save His people from destruction **(Ezekiel 22:30)**.

As spiritual conflicts rage on with more tenacity in our contemporary society, we must go back to the ministry of intercession. We intercede through prayer, petitioning for others before the throne of God. You can wage a mighty battle of intercessory prayer.

How often do you pray? How much time have you invested into your prayer life? Most Christians don't pray five times a month— and only then because they are in trouble. This is why they live such defeated lives. The enemy wants you to live a prayerless life. He knows that you would be too hot for him to handle if you continue to pray. How can you resist the devil without prayer? John Wesley said that it seems God can do nothing unless somebody prays. He was correct!

LET US PRAY!

1. Reflect on how this reflection on *"Prayer and Fasting"* ministers to you.

2. Pray and ask God for the forgiveness of your sins using **Psalm 51.**

3. Put on the full armor of God by praying *"The Warrior's Prayer"* (see page 18).

4. Pray *"The Act of Spiritual Communion"* prayer (see page 19).

5. Pray **Psalm 43** (a prayer to God in time of trouble).

6. Acknowledge that you cannot really pray without the help of the Holy Spirit **(Romans 8:26)**. In the name of Jesus Christ, ask the Holy Spirit to:
   a. Breathe upon you the Spirit of prayer;
   b. Wear you the garment of prayer;
   c. Make you pray like Jesus;
   d. Make you a prayer-addict from today;
   e. Help you grow spiritually;
   f. Use your prayer to bring revival or spiritual awakening in your land;
   g. Use your prayer to enkindle the fire of prayer in your family;
   h. Keep the fire of prayer always burning in your life;
   i. Help you pray with the Word of God.

7. Ask the Holy Spirit to use your prayers to:
   a. Grow your intercessory strength;
   b. Grow your relationship with God;
   c. Grow your knowledge of God;
   d. Grow your worship life;
   e. Grow and shape your godly character.

8. The prayers of Jesus were heartfelt supplication, demonstrating empathy and a genuine love for God. He prayed for Himself, His immediate disciples, as well as for all believers **(John 17:1-26)**.
   a. Ask Holy Spirit to help make your prayers to be motivated by a deep and a genuine love for God;
   b. Ask God to help you pray in the way that pleases Him;
   c. Like Jesus, pray for all believers. *(Ask the Holy Spirit to bring to your mind the needs to pray for. Spend some time here in prayer).*

9. Thank You Lord Jesus Christ for answering my prayers. I cover this prayer with the Most Precious Blood of Jesus Christ (7 times).

DAY 19 - Part 2: Warfare Prayers

Note:

- Reflect on what John Chrysostom (347-407 AD) had to say about the power of prayer: *"Prayer is an all-efficient panoply [i.e. 'a full suit of armor' or 'splendid array'], a treasure undiminished, a mind never exhausted, a sky unobstructed by clouds, a haven unruffled by storm. It is the root, the fountain, and the mother of a thousand blessings. It exceeds a monarch's power... I speak not of the prayer which is cold and feeble and devoid of zeal. I speak of that which proceeds from a mind outstretched, the child of a contrite spirit, the offspring of a soul converted - this is the prayer which mounts to heaven... The power of prayer has subdued the strength of fire, bridled the rage of lions, silenced anarchy, extinguished wars, appeased the elements, expelled demons, burst the chains of death, enlarged the gates of heaven, relieved diseases, averted frauds, rescued cities from destruction, stayed the sun in its course, and arrested the progress of the thunderbolt. In essence, prayer has the power to destroy whatever is at enmity with the good."*

- Is God asking you to intercede for a person, a nation or an area of breakthrough? Is He asking you to be the one to stand in the gap for the land?

1. Praise and worship God as the Holy Spirit leads you.

2. Pray **Psalm 51**. Use it to ask for God's forgiveness of your sins.

3. Put on the full armor of God by praying "The Warrior's Prayer" (see page 18).

4. Pray "The Act of Spiritual Communion" prayer (see page 19).

5. I decree that nothing can stand against my prayer, in the name of Jesus Christ.

6. Holy Spirit, pray through me the will of the Father.

7. Holy Spirit, help me to always want to pray more effectively, in the name of Jesus Christ.

8. Holy Spirit, help me never to give up praying about any situation until God's power comes into it, in the name of Jesus Christ.

9. **Psalm 107:13-14** says, *"Then they cried to the Lord in their trouble, and He saved them from their distress; He brought them out of darkness and gloom, and broke their bonds asunder."* While praying in the name of Jesus Christ:
   a. Now begin to bring your troubles to God;
   b. Like Abraham, pray for the problems of others (and for nations of the world). Spend some time here (ask the Holy Spirit to bring to your mind things to pray for);
   c. Like Moses, pray for Government leaders to become God-fearing people.

10. In the name of Jesus Christ, let this prayer:
   a. Bring me personal deliverance over satanic forces;
   b. Bring me victory and multiple breakthroughs;
   c. Arrest all the spirits causing delayed miracles in my life;
   d. Revoke every evil decree over my life;
   e. Help me to mount up with wings as eagles;
   f. Paralyze every deeply-rooted problem that I am going through;
   g. Uproot every tree of non-achievement;
   h. Destroy every household wickedness;
   i. Deliver me from ancestral bondage;
   j. Remove blockages operating at the edge of miracles;
   k. Destroy every satanic network operating against my life;
   l. Demolish stumbling blocks on my way;
   m. Lead me to God's will concerning the issue I am praying about;
   n. Bring forth my desired healing;
   o. Unseat every strongman sitting on my godly inheritance;

p. Bring forth divine elevation, miraculous openings, and restoration in my life;

q. Disgrace every spirit that has been disgracing me (and my people);

r. Enable me to tread upon the serpents and scorpions;

s. Make all people of God receive fresh fire from Heaven;

t. Arrest and crush the spirits causing conflicts and hostility in homes;

u. Free my children and loved ones from bondage;

v. Destroy every evil covenant and evil altars in my bloodline;

w. Roll away every stone of limitations placed on my life;

x. Reveal the secret behind what I am passing through;

y. Enkindle in me the fire of God's love;

z. Give me a great testimony.

11. **Reflection:** Jesus taught persistence in prayer **(Luke 18:1)**. However, not all our prayers would be answered as expected. Even Jesus prayed three times for God to take away the bitter cup of suffering, but it was the Father's will that His Son would have to drink it **(Matthew 26:36-44)**. However, Jesus prayed for His Father's will to be done. Here, Jesus offered tremendous but seemingly simple insight into prayer. Like Jesus, we ought to submit to God's will.

12. Thank You, Lord Jesus Christ, for the gift of prayer and intercession.

13. I cover this prayer with the Most Precious Blood of Jesus Christ (7 times)

Chapter 10

The Angels of God

"Then the Angel of the Lord set out and struck down one hundred eighty-five thousand in the camp of the Assyrians; when morning dawned, they were all dead bodies"

(Isaiah 37:36)

[Other suggested Bible passages to read:
Revelation 12:7-11, Daniel 10:1-14, Acts 12:1-11, Psalm 91:11-12,
Luke 1:26-38, Exodus 23:20-21, Psalm 103:20-21].

DAY 20 - Part 1: Reflection

Angels are powerful weapons of warfare! We need angelic security and artillery! The Scripture depicts God's Angels as being directly involved in spiritual conflicts: *"And war broke out in heaven; Michael and his Angels fought against the dragon. The dragon and his angels fought back"* (**Revelation 12:7**).

One of the ways that Angels become involved in the spiritual battle we find ourselves is through our prayers. When Daniel prayed and fasted for 21 days, it was his prayers that brought his victory as Archangel Michael came to fight for him (**Daniel 10:1-14**). When Peter was put in prison, it was the prayer of the Church that resulted in God sending an Angel to Peter to break him free from prison **(Acts 12:1-11)**. Several references in the Scriptures highlight the salient truth that as we pray and intercede, the Lord sends Angels into the affairs of His people on earth. This is one of the rules in spiritual engagements!

So, we too do have a role to play in how Angels are released and engaged in spiritual operations of warfare. Prayer is so powerful because it determines the outcome of things in the physical world. The victory that plays out in the physical is the result of the victory attained in the spiritual world.

So, we need the ministry or services of the Angels of God in the art of spiritual warfare. Even Jesus received the ministry of Angels during His Ministry on earth. After His conflict with the devil in the wilderness for 40 days, *"Then the devil left Him, and behold, Angels came and ministered to Him"* (Matthew 4:11). In **Luke 22:43**, *"An Angel appeared to Him from heaven, strengthening Him"* (NKJV). If the ministry of Angels was necessary for Jesus, then it very much necessary for us as well.

You see, no one is as anointed as Jesus, yet He needed the services of the Angels. A Christian writer once said, *"The anointing cannot replace the services of the Angels."* That is true! **Acts 10:38** testifies that *"God anointed Jesus of Nazareth with the Holy Spirit and with power,"* yet it took an Angel of the Lord to roll back the stone that sealed Jesus' tomb on the day of resurrection **(Matthew 28:2)**.

My dear, listen: There are closed doors in your life that only Angels of God can open. There are obstacles, mountains or stones in your life that only Angels of God can roll away before you can experience the victory you are seeking. There are heights you cannot attain, and there are destinies you cannot reach without the Angels of God. There are blessings you cannot get, there are fights you cannot fight alone and win; there are messages you cannot get directly from God, there are stones you cannot roll away on our own, and there are many more things you cannot do— except by the help of the Angels of God!

The message cannot be made clearer: There are exploits which we cannot accomplish by anointing but by the ministry of Angels. God created Angels not only to serve Him but to help us. He even assigned to each one of us a "guardian Angel" to protect and guide us **(Psalm 91:11-12)**. We need the ministry of Angels to live a victorious Christian life.

It is a serious crack on the wall when we ignore to invite God's Angels during warfare. It took Archangel Michael to bring victory to Daniel as he engaged in his 21-day warfare prayer. We ought to invite the Angels during spiritual engagements: Michael (the minister of defense), Gabriel (the minister of good news), Raphael (the minister of healing), and the other untold millions of angels in heaven.

These Angels are spirits in your divine service! **Hebrews 1:14** says, *"Are not all Angels spirits in the divine service, sent to serve for the sake of those who are to inherit salvation?"* My dear friend, you are a candidate to inherit the salvation of God, and God has deployed His Angels to lead you into your heritage.

The Lord promises in **Exodus 33:2** saying, *"I will send an angel before you, and I will drive out the Canaanites, the Amorites, the Hittites, the Perizzites, the Hivites, and the Jebusites."* Do you notice that it was only one Angel of God that drove away the enemies occupying the land of Israel's heritage? This still happens today as the Lord dispatches His Angels to drive out the tyrant enemies occupying the land of blessings that He has given to us.

2 Kings 19:35 says, *"That very night the Angel of the Lord set out and struck down one hundred eighty-five thousand in the camp of* *the Assyrians; when morning dawned, they were all dead bodies."* Again, do you notice that it was just one Angel that slew 185,000 Assyrians— armies for that matter, not civilians? Moreover, 2 **Chronicles 32:21** says, *"And the Lord sent an Angel who cut off all the mighty warriors and commanders and officers in the camp of the king of Assyria. So he returned in disgrace to his own land."*

Furthermore, in the Book of Revelations, John testifies that he *"saw an Angel coming down from heaven, holding in his hand the key to the bottomless pit and a great chain. He seized the dragon, that ancient serpent, who is the devil and Satan, and bound him for a thousand years, and threw him into the pit, and locked and sealed it over him"* **(Revelation 20:1-3).** These are not coincidences but a testament to how powerful and mighty God's Angels are.

Can you imagine one of these Angels fighting for you! Surely, God is waiting for you to ask Him to release His Angels to fight against your spiritual enemies. We see in these verses just how powerful and mighty one Angel of the Lord is. Think about this one Angel that slew 185,000 of the Assyrian army in one night coming to fight your own battle. This is what the Lord will do for you as you hand over the situation to Him. The Lord will surely make your spiritual enemies be *"like chaff before the wind, with the Angel of the Lord driving them away"* **(Psalm 35:5).**

Angels have specific areas in which they specialize in their operations. For example, St. Michael the Archangel, is known for protecting God's people from evil, temptations, harm, or from spiritual attacks in general. This highlights the beauty of praying the St. Michael the Archangel prayer every day in the course of this prayer (and even as a daily prayer). He will help you in weathering the storm of life.

Similarly, Archangel Raphael specializes in healing, while Archangel Gabriel brings good news to people. However, God knows exactly which Angel is the right one to help you in your struggles. You may be calling on Archangel Michael to help you and protect you, but protection may not be what you need. You might actually need guidance or healing. In that case, God sends Archangel Raphael whose very name means "God heals" or "healing power of God."

As we are drawing the curtain on this chapter, I wish to encourage you to get the Angels of God involved in your spiritual engagements. Remember, the testimony of God's people when they were in a horrible situation: *"when we cried to the Lord, He heard our voice, and sent an Angel and brought us out of Egypt"* (**Numbers 20:16**). Cry to the Lord in prayer and He will send forth His Angels to deliver you.

If you feel like you are sinking, know that the Angels of the living God will help keep your head out of the deep waters. They will not let you get drowned, but you have the responsibility to keep "swimming" to the shore with your prayers!

LET US PRAY!
1. Reflect on how this reflection on *"The Angels of God"* ministers to you.

2. Pray and ask God for the forgiveness of your sins using **Psalm 51.**

3. Put on the full armor of God by praying *"The Warrior's Prayer"* (see page 18).

4. Pray *"The Act of Spiritual Communion"* prayer (see page 19).

5. Pray **Psalm 91** for God's Protection (Reflect on Verse 5-6: *"For He will command His Angels concerning you to guard you in all your ways. On their hands, they will bear you up, so that you will not dash your foot against a stone"*).

6. In the name of Jesus Christ, call on God's Angels for protection and ministering. Lord Jesus Christ, please, send Your...
   a. Holy and Mighty Angels to surround us in this prayer. Let Your Angels drive out every unclean spirit from here and send them to the foot of the Cross;
   b. Ministering Angels, Your healing Angels, and Your warring Angels to keep us safe in all our ways.

7. Let the Angels of God break every chain holding my life down, in the name of Jesus Christ. Continue praying, in the name of Jesus Christ:
   a. O Lord Jesus, as You deployed an Angel to deliver captive Peter when chained in prison by Herod **(Acts 12:3-11)**, so may You send Your Angels to break every chain tying me down in spiritual prison:
      i. Lord Jesus, release me from every spiritual chain;
      ii. Lord Jesus, bring me safely out of every spiritual prison.
   b. Pray strongly, asking the Angels of God to walk in your bloodline to break every ancestral cord tying everyone down to stagnation.

8. Let the Angels of God deliver me from the horrible pit of death, in the name of Jesus Christ. Continue praying, in the name of Jesus Christ:
   a. O Lord God, as You sent Your Angel to deliver Daniel from the pit packed with hungry lions **(Daniel 6:22)**, so may You dispatch Your Angels to deliver me from the pit of death;
   b. O Lord God, as You sent an Angel to deliver Shedrack, Mishark, and Abednego from the burning fire, so may I ask of You to send Your Angels to deliver me from every fiery fire I am going through right now.

9. Thank You Lord Jesus Christ for answering my prayers. I cover this prayer with the Most Precious Blood of Jesus Christ (7 times).

THE ANGELS OF GOD

DAY 21 - Part 2: Warfare Prayers

Note:

- In the battle that we face against the kingdom of darkness, God has not left us without help. He has given us Angels to help us. Angels are our chief weapons in the arena of spiritual warfare.

- Remember that you are not alone in the battle you find yourself if you invite God into it! The Holy Spirit is inside you and the Angels are around you. As you call on God, you will expect a release of His Angels on your behalf!

- The Lord God promises, *"I am going to send an Angel in front of you, to guard you on the way and to bring you to the place that I have prepared"* (Exodus 23:20).

- So, let your prayers activate God's Holy Angels on assignment to fight for you!

1. Praise and worship God as the Holy Spirit leads you.

2. Pray **Psalm 51** for God's forgiveness of your sins.

3. Put on the full armor of God by praying *"The Warrior's Prayer"* (see page 18).

4. Pray *"The Act of Spiritual Communion" prayer (see page 19).*

5. Pray the *"Guardian Angel Prayer"*: *"Angel of God, my guardian dear, to whom God's love commits me here, ever this day be at my side, to light and guard, to rule and guide. Amen!"*

6. O Lord God, as You stationed Your troop of Angels at the frontiers of Elisha's seminary when the Arameans came to attack him **(2 Kings 6:17)**, so may You station Your hosts of Angels to defend me and my family from every advancing enemy—I pray in the name of Jesus Christ.

7. I arm myself with angelic armies, in the name of Jesus Christ. I confess that I am surrounded by God's Angels.

8. Pray for an angelic touch of healing in your life and in the lives of your loved ones. Talk to God concerning areas you need healing *(pray in the name of Jesus Christ)*.

9. Pray for an angelic touch of healing in the lives of people who are sick *(pray in the name of Jesus Christ)*:
   a. Lord Jesus, I ask You to send forth Your Angels to minister a healing touch to everyone who is sick:
      i. Let Your people rise from their deathbeds completely healed;
      ii. I pray that many will experience a special angelic touch that will heal them in spirit, soul, and body;
      iii. Pray for people who are being attacked by evil spirits (nightmare, demonic apparitions, suicide spirits, evil manipulations, and all forms of deceptions). Let the Angels give them a touch of deliverance.
   b. Pray for people who are living in bondage. Let the Angels locate them so they receive a message of truth that will set them free, and lead them down the path of repentance, and back into the loving arms of the heavenly Father.

10. Pray the following, in the name of Jesus Christ, for angelic deliverance. Lord Jesus Christ:
   a. Thank You for giving Your Angels charge over me to deliver me from troubles **(Psalm 91:11)**;
   b. Hear my voice and send Your angels to deliver me from the hand of the enemy **(Numbers 20:16)**;
   c. Let Your Angels ascend and descend upon my life **(Genesis 28:12)**. May they ascend with my petitions and descend upon me with answered prayers;
   d. Let Your Angel chase and persecute my enemies **(Psalm 35:5-6)**;
   e. Let Your Angels fight for me in the heavens against

principalities and powers in the high places **(Daniel 10:13)**;

    f.   Let the Angel of Your Presence go before me to make the crooked places in my life straight **(Isaiah 63:9)**.

11.   Begin to make the following confessions (in the name of Jesus Christ):

    a.   I have come to Zion, surrounded by an innumerable company of Angels **(Hebrews 12:22)**;

    b.   The Angels shall stand by me to minister to me in the day and in the night **(Acts 27:23)**;

    c.   The Angels shall meet me as I walk in my destiny **(Genesis 32:1)**;

    d.   The Angels are already smiting the demons that have come to destroy me, my family, and Ministry;

    e.   The Angels are accompanying me in reaching out to the lost and to those in need of godly enlightenment **(Acts 8:26)**;

    f.   The Angels are fighting and defending the Church.

12.   People, sometimes, talk about others as if they were angels. They are normal humans but behave angelic. This is because, although human, such people have the qualities of God's Angels. Such a person sent to your life is your destiny helper!

    a.   Pray for God to send destiny helpers your way;

    b.   Pray for your destiny helpers.

13.   I refuse to let my Angels of blessings depart from me, in the name of Jesus Christ.

14.   Let my Angels of blessings drive away every power blowing away my blessings, in the name of Jesus Christ.

15.   Let my Angels of blessings recover all my stolen blessings, in the name of Jesus Christ.

16.   Lord Jesus Christ, thank You for sending Your Angels to minister peace and encouragement to me, and to deliver me

from every work of the enemies. I Thank You, Lord Jesus:

    a. For Your Angels that watch over me every time;

    b. For sending the Angels to shut every lion's mouth that has been set on my way to devour me;

    c. For sending Your Angels to remind us of Your love and deliver warnings in time of dangers.

17. I cover this prayer with the Most Precious Blood of Jesus Christ (7 times).

Epilogue

Think. Think. I say, think! Think of one thing that God is telling you after reading this book. Could HE be asking you, "Where are your armor and Weapons?" Suppose God asked this question to a tortoise, it would rightly respond, "I carry my armor-shell wherever I go. The ants or bees would say, "We carry our stinging weapons everywhere. The scorpion would respond, "I carry the poison you gave me to protect myself." So would the lions, porcupines, snakes, spiders, bulls, and so on. They all carry their weapons all the time: whether eating, playing, sleeping, or hunting. They don't drop their Weapons. They understand that their survival is tied to using their weapons and knowing how to use them.

Regrettably, as for many people of God—people who God created in His own image—they have dropped their armor and weapons meant to protect them from being casualties in the hands of the devil and his kingdom of darkness. Let us go to the ants or the scorpions and learn how to be battle-ready, always carrying our weapons!

In answering this question, I hope you are not among the countless Christians who have dropped their spiritual weapons and armor. I pray this book motivates you to be like the bees: always armed and dangerous! Always ready to fight!

The difference between a victor and a victim lies in whether you carry your armor and weapons with you all the time (not just some time) or not. *The Warrior's Weapons* has expounded the spiritual weapons. Use your weapons! Use them always! Use this book! Get it for your children and friends.

God bless you!

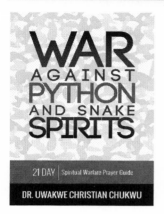

War Against Python and Snake Spirits

The first Biblical prophecy in Genesis 3:15 simply reveals a salient truth: There is a spiritual hostility and conflict between the righteous and the devil, the ancient serpent. God wants us to engage the ancient serpent in a battle. He wants us to use the authority He has given to us to smash the serpent's head! Unfortunately, so many people of God are bound by demonic forces but do not know how to be free. The proliferation of python and snake spirits in this end time has resulted in an epidemic of people living in spiritual bondage. These python and snake spirits have aggressive appetite for destinies to swallow! War Against Python And Snake Spirits is an attempt to address this problem.

The Warrior's Weapons (Volume 1 & 2)

Never in the history of mankind has there been an era of war like ours. We could smell war in the air. While the media reminds us of physical wars, the struggles we go through everyday remind us of spiritual wars. In a sense, it seems that there is an outbreak of demonic hostilities. Now that we know that we are at war, so what? What are we going to do about it? If we are to survive these trying times in which we live, it is imperative that we learn how to effectively use the weapons of warfare against the devil and his companions. In this book, you have everything you need to become armed and dangerous against every adversary that threatens you and your destiny. The book presents some strategic weapons from our spiritual arsenal and how they are to be used against the kingdom of darkness.

The Invisible War (Volume 1 & 2)

Spiritual war is a fierce battle that is not visible to the ordinary eyes. The war is invisible, but the impact is real. All of us are in the midst of this war which rages underneath the earth, inside the waters, in the air, and in the heavenlies. The battle goes on irrespective of whether we know it or not, or whether we believe it or not. There is no break in the war, no causal leave, and no cease-fire! This occurs every single day both during the day and night. The Invisible War is a fire-loaded warfare book prayerfully packaged to make you dangerous against every spiritual adversary that threatens your destiny. It is written to be engaging as you find in it a blend of real-life experiences, history, Scriptures, storytelling, and prayers.

Made in the USA
Columbia, SC
09 September 2019